Dear Tanya -

I can't thank you enough for getting me back to the "BHB" after all these years! Couldn't do it without you! It is TRULY a special place and you are TRULY a special person and dear friend -

lots of love
Ru

June 2016

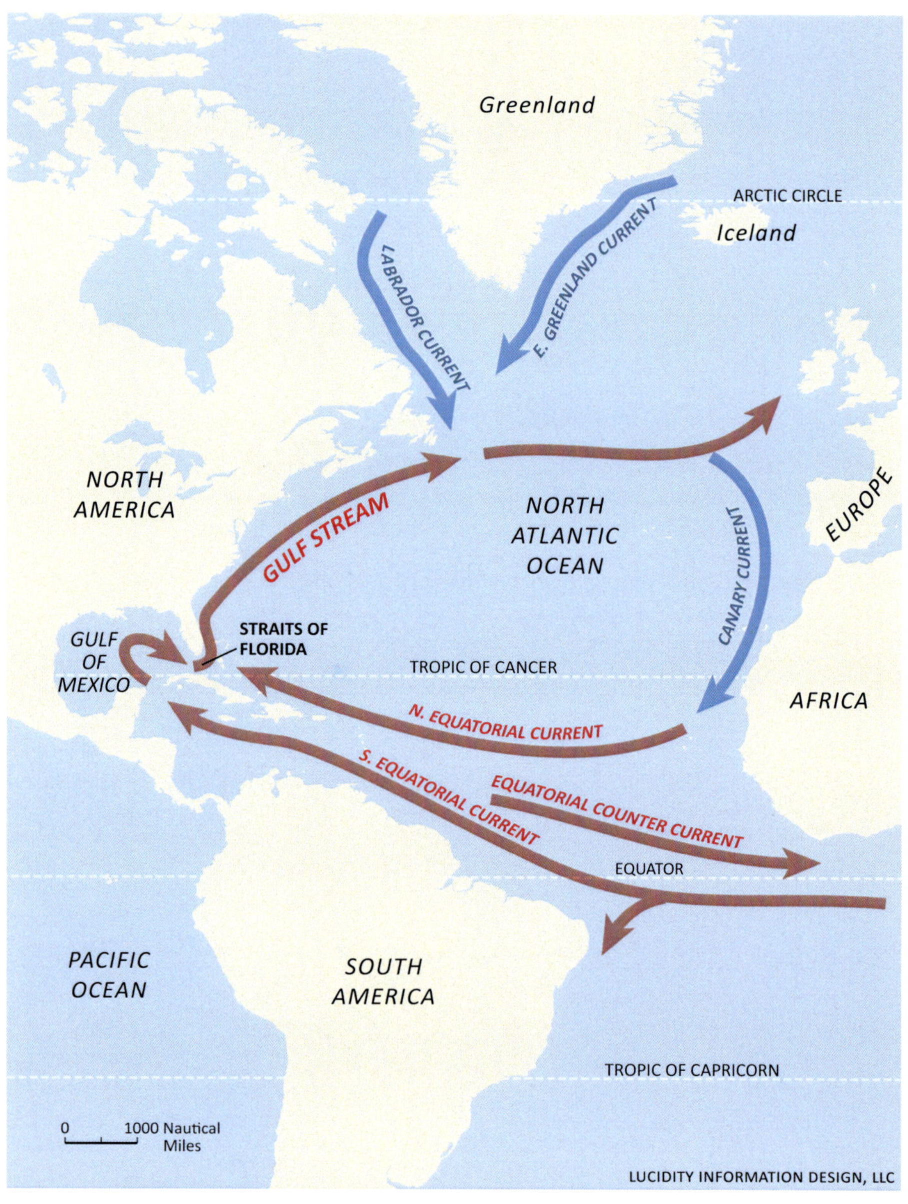

ISBN 978-0-692-31211-7 US $44.95
Library of Congress #1-822115801

Published and Distributed by Ocean Art Publications,
div. of NiTe Flight Photo Graphics, Boca Raton, FL (561) 394-6391

About the Gulf Stream Current

Over the years, the Blue Heron Bridge has gained notoriety on an international scale as one of the top muck dives in the world. A muck dive means, it may not necessarily be a pretty site with flowing sea fans and colorful reefs, as it affected by tidal exchanges pushing tanic waters from inner canals, fresh water run off and the debris it may carry in during heavy storms. This exchange attracts an unusual assortment of marine life.

A number of factors contribute to the unique underwater life found here. Located inside Florida's Intra-Coastal Waterway, close to the Lake Worth Inlet and it's close proximity to the Gulf Stream Current which runs north along the Eastern Seaboard of the United States, marine life finds it's way into this "shallow nursery" of sorts, to propagate, visit or sustain new life. To understand the diversity of life we see here, understanding a little about the enormity of travel encompassed by this current is helpful in perhaps seeing the bigger picture.

The Gulf Stream Current was first discovered in the early 1500's by Ponce de Leon. The current begins flowing off the west coast of North Africa, where it joins the Atlantic North Equatorial current, that flows from the African continent across the Atlantic Ocean. Once it reaches the eastern edge of South America, the current splits into two currents, one being the Antilles Current. These currents are funneled through the islands of the Caribbean and through the Yucatan Channel. These areas are narrow, causing the current to compress and gather strength. As it circulates into the Gulf of Mexico's warm waters, it is here that the Gulf Stream becomes visible by satellite, and is believed that this is where the Gulf Stream current actually originates.

From the Gulf of Mexico, the Gulf Stream Current moves east, rejoins the Antilles Current and exits through the Straits of Florida (at the southern most tip of Florida). It is a powerful underwater river that is known to transport water at the rate of 30 million cubic meters per second, traveling at speeds of up to 120 kilometers per day, and can extend to 1,000 meters below the surface. It then flows north, parallel to the east coast of the United States, then veers into open ocean near Cape Hatteras, North Carolina. It has to be one heck of a ride for sea creatures, like the EAC in Australia seen in the movie "NEMO." The Lake Worth Inlet that leads to the Blue Heron Bridge, juts out somewhat, into the Gulf Stream as it waivers in and out, bringing with it a host of unusual characters to this natural marine sanctuary.

Ribbon Cutting Ceremony Grand Opening

With the park & bridge improvements completed, more and more folks flocked to the park and it soon became evident that further measures would be needed to keep a happy balance between boaters, fishermen, divers, snorkelers and swimmers. The divers, underwater photographers and scientists had discovered a plethora under the horizon. The first initiative was to determine what would be necessary to have this area converted to a Protected Marine Sanctuary. After a public town meeting, this idea was quickly squashed.

Our thought was, if they can accommodate tourists, boaters, divers, and fishermen in the Keys, we can figure out a way to do this here! We soon came to a solution that it would be very beneficial to create an artificial reef; a.) as a barrier and underwater demarcation between the diving areas and the boating channel, b.) to attract even more marine life, c.) insert flotation markers that boaters could easily see with signage in the water to indicate no boats beyond a certain point, which therefore then would d.) create a protected area for swimmers, snorkelers and divers, e.) improve the snorkeling and diving experiences.

Left to Right: Councilmember Judy L. Davis, City of Riviera Beach, Rob Robbins, Director, Palm Beach County Dept. Environmental Resources Mgt, Commissioner Priscilla A. Taylor, PB County Commisioners, Councilmember Billie E. Brooks

New Snorkel and Dive Trail at Phil Foster Park

I am proud that I was asked to join this committee a few years ago, led at that time by Palm Beach County Commissioner Karen Marcus. The committee had several members from Parks & Recreation, the Department of Environmental Resources, Shana & Dean Phelan from Pura Vida Divers, representing the South Florida Recreational Diving Operators & the City of Riviera Beach. With all the recent hub-ub about this being named a world class muck site, and gaining so much attention from international divers and photographers, the county realized the importance of developing and protecting this area. "We have to raise public awareness."

Much to my delight, my first book, "Under the Bridge," was a motivating factor that grabbed the attention of the county and was used as the "proof-of-life" documentary by the committee to gain the state funding for this beautiful snorkel trail. Our underwater world is very important. As the reef takes hold and spawns new incredible life, and the public becomes more aware of this unusual marine habitat, perhaps further steps can be initiated to make this a "designated dive" area in the future. We are so fortunate to have this wonder in our back yard!

Left to Right: Eric Call, Director Palm Beach County Parks & Recreation, Suzan Meldonian, Author of Under the Bridge, Commissioner Karen Marcus, PBC Board of Commissioners, Evelyn DuPlecy, Staff Assistant to Representative Jeff Clemens, Dan Liftman, Staff Assistant to U.S. Congress Representative Alcee Hastings.

August 2012

Acknowledgments

Special acknowledgments to Force-E Dive Centers and Pura Vida Divers here in Florida for all their continued support and encouragement, and all their lovely staff and for making the night dives possible. Special thanks to George Burgess at the Florida Museum of Natural History, Coordinator of Museum Operations, Director, Florida Program for Shark Research Curator, who decided to document our photo finds, and whose fish identification and validation contributed greatly to the success and implementation of the new artificial Reef and Snorkel Trail at Phil Foster Park.

Special thanks goes also to Andre C. Morandini, PhD, Assist. Professor, Departamento de Zoologia, Instituto de Biociências, Instituto de Biociências, Universidade de São Paulo, Brazil for his assistance on Jellyfish id's; Anne DuPont and Linda Ianniello for their continued help on identifications with nudibranchs and sea slugs, Bill Frank and Harry G. Lee at Jax Shells.org, and a tremendous gratitude to Les Wilk, Paul Humann, Anne & Ned Deloach for their wonderful marine life identification books.

Credits:
Photo Editor: Suzan Meldonian
Illustrations: Lucidity Information Design, LLC
Layout & Design: Ocean Art Publications, div .of NiTe Flight Photo Graphics
Publisher: NiTe Flight Photo Graphics
First Edition 2014 Copyright 2014

PHOTO CREDITS

Ribbon Cutting, Alyssa Dodd ii; Octopus with eggs, Deb Devers 130, Micro Photography of Nematocyst, Waldo Nell 83; Golden Mantis, André Johnson 241; Mustache Jawfish Kelly Casey, 15; Photo of Suzan Meldonian, Bernd Meier; Sargassumfish, 216, Cuthona caerulea, 234, Red Orange Ghost Shrimp 241, Oscellated & Striated Frogfish with colors orange, yellow, mauve 218-219, Linda Ianniello. All other images photographed by Suzan Meldonian.

ISBN-10:0692312110
ISBN-13:978-0-692-31211-7

THE BHB

An Underwater Marine Life Guide of the Blue Heron Bridge

What you might see at the BHB!

If all you see when you look at the sea is nothing more than a mere blue horizon line, while you may find solace in its expanse, you have no idea of the complexity of the life cycles that abound and flourish below. Entire communities proliferate, living in harmony, symbiotically keeping their own balance within nature.

Perhaps there is something to be witnessed, something to be learned by us, their neighbors above. Take memories and leave only bubbles.

Dedicated to all the citizen scientists with a curiosity to observe marine wildlife in the rough. Protecting our oceans begins with our own evolutionary education of the delicate balance between land, sea and mankind. Get involved. Learn. Teach.

I dare you not to be amazed.

Diving at the Blue Heron Bridge requires strict adherence to the tide tables, which can be found on the NOAA site or tide tables (such as produced by Sea Tow) or may be obtained at the local dive shops.
See Index for links.

Plan your dive to begin 1 hour before high tide (slack tide).
Allow ample time for parking and time to gear up.
Although this is an "easy" shallow beach dive, the tidal current sweeping through here can be extreme at the full and new moon intervals. Caution and attention to this is necessary as strong currents can be dangerous outside a 2 hour window. You don't want to be swept into the boat channel. Diving in a current can be exhausting. Trying to swim back against the current is not advised.

A Dive Flag is required.
No diving in the Channel -it's dangerous- really.

Night Diving is only allowed with Permitted Dive operations when the tide tables coincide with the Park's 10:00 PM curfew.
The following dive operators conduct Permitted Night Dives at the Bridge:

Force E Dive Center, Riviera Beach
Pura Vida Divers, Riviera Beach
Bottom Time Boat, Riviera Beach

This area is considered to be a "No-Take" Zone - Please no harvesting!
3mm wetsuit is recommended in summer May- October
5mm wetsuit is recommended in winter October-April
The deepest depth at high tide is 23' - extra weights are necessary

photo: Sand Perch Screaming- no more pictures!

If you know what you are looking for, you will find it.

Many new divers will experience their first open water dives at the BHB. At first it may not seem particularly exciting to look at. There are not any beautiful purple sea fans flowing in the breeze, or massive coral reefs. But take a minute. Stop. Lie still on the sandy bottom and just observe. Be quiet and calm, and the little people of the sea will breathe back into their space, almost as if you are not there. Suddenly you might see timid Garden eels pop their heads up out of their holes from the corner of your eye. Spotted Eagle Rays are known to frequent the area and are always a treat to behold as they gracefully fly past you. Fish with feet may wobble along the sea floor, or you might get lucky to see a Stargazer explode from its camouflaged hide-away in the sand.

Manatees, sometimes pass through, and are magnificent to behold (to see something that large in the water with you can be breath-taking). Keep in mind they are protected- so please don't try to touch them. Just observe. Don't want to scare them away.

With all sea life . . . respect their space. Most sea life has a slippery coating, which protects them from infection or illness. So, please don't touch the animals. Manhandling sea life to get a photo is just not cool at all. You will get your best shots sitting still waiting for the moment and studying the animal's behavior. Wait for it ...

This is a very silty area, work on your buoyancy control, and try finning frog kick style. It's great exercise for the inner thighs. Gently- there's no rush. it makes for snowy looking photos, not to mention, it can wreck the water clarity for your buddies behind you. Time your dive to get you back in front of the beach area after about an hour to avoid strong currents that can perk up without warning on either side of the island.

Plan your dive on the incoming tide= 1 hour before High Tide. Be mindful of your flag line, as it is easy to get hung up on the bridge pilings or other diver's flag lines. Cylumes are used on the flags for permitted night dives.

Brown Garden Eel, *Heteroconger longissimus*

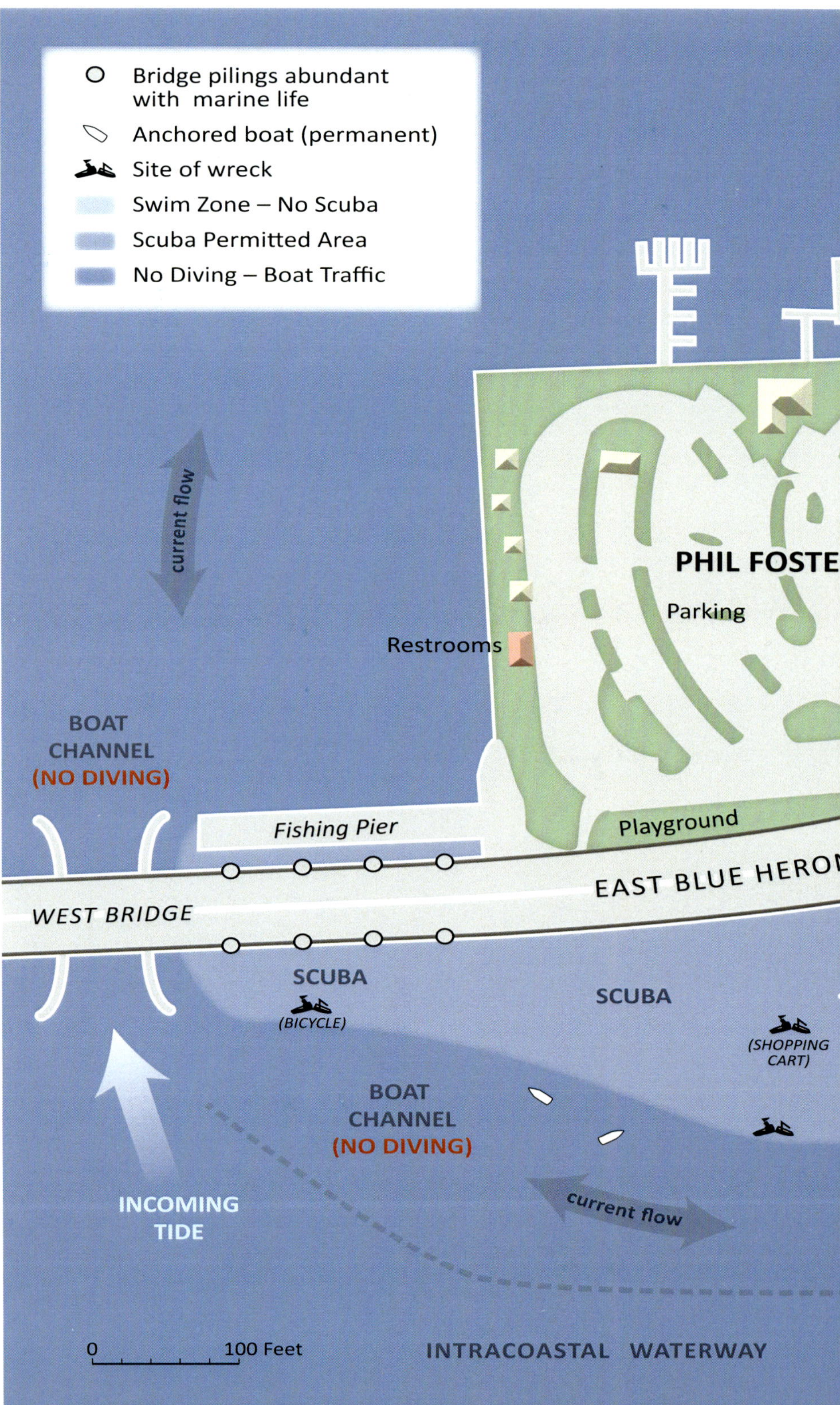

Bridge pilings abundant with marine life
Anchored boat (permanent)
Site of wreck
Swim Zone – No Scuba
Scuba Permitted Area
No Diving – Boat Traffic
current flow
PHIL FOSTER
Parking
Restrooms
BOAT CHANNEL (NO DIVING)
Fishing Pier
Playground
EAST BLUE HERON
WEST BRIDGE
SCUBA
(BICYCLE)
SCUBA
(SHOPPING CART)
BOAT CHANNEL (NO DIVING)
INCOMING TIDE
current flow
0
100 Feet
INTRACOASTAL WATERWAY

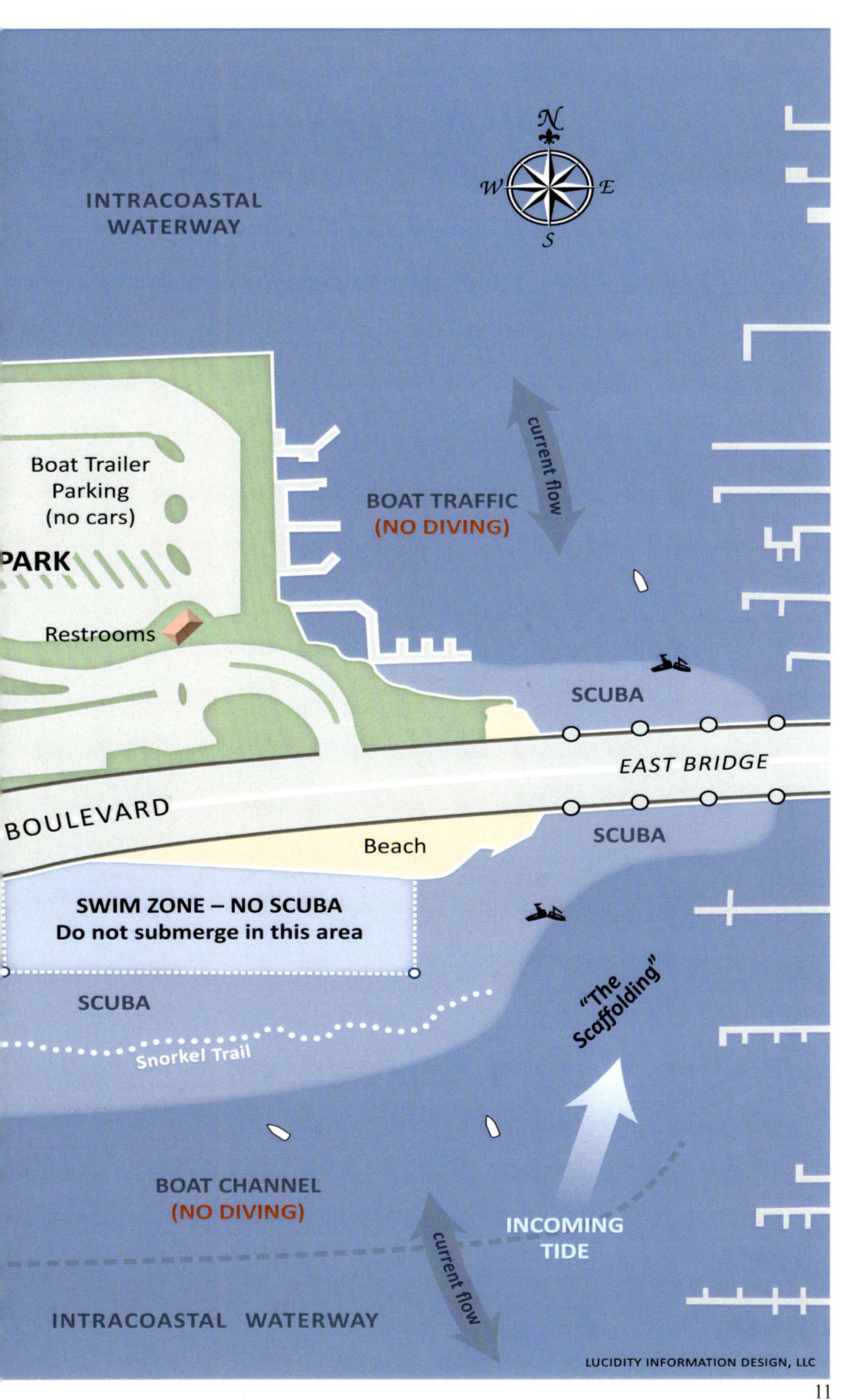
N
W
E
S
INTRACOASTAL
WATERWAY
Boat Trailer
Parking
(no cars)
PARK
Restrooms
current flow
BOAT TRAFFIC
(NO DIVING)
SCUBA
EAST BRIDGE
BOULEVARD
Beach
SCUBA
SWIM ZONE – NO SCUBA
Do not submerge in this area
SCUBA
Snorkel Trail
"The
Scaffolding"
BOAT CHANNEL
(NO DIVING)
current flow
INCOMING
TIDE
INTRACOASTAL WATERWAY
LUCIDITY INFORMATION DESIGN, LLC

Welcome to my world!

This book has been organized in a variety of manners to assist new divers in identifying something that they saw with little or no knowledge of the critter. But & also for the seasoned divers who have seen it all; but can't remember what it is called.

Therefore you will find sections by colors, dots and stripes, and of course we have included a dangerous marine life section to help keep you safe by raising your awareness of the multitude of stinging creatures that frequent the Blue Heron Bridge.

Most of these creatures can be seen anywhere in our Atlantic & Caribbean backyards, but I doubt you could see so many different creatures in one concentrated area if it is not on a muck dive.

Photo: Sailfin Blenny waving hello, *Emblemaria pandionis*, male

CONTENTS:

A pair of mating Downey Blennies, Labrisomus kalisherae, snuggle and romp around like two little kittens with a ball of yarn, only stopping once or twice to see if you are still there. This may go on for well over thirty minutes. They are much larger than Seaweed Blennies. Perhaps 6-8”

Photo tip:

Behavior shots can be much more interesting than portrait shots and to witness our undersea friends eating, fighting, showing off, flirting, building a house, or even building a sand ball is an incredible experience to behold. Most certainly focus on catching their eye glint in your image. It gives depth of perception and creates a connection between the subject and the observer.

COURTSHIP & MATING BEHAVIORS

If you want to get pictures of fish doing unusual things- Dusky Jawfish, Opistognathus whitehursti, are a constant source of entertainment. Ranging in size from the size of your pinky finger to the size of your fist... they blend in well with their surroundings, keep an eye out for specific movement that opposes the water current. This fellow is building his burrow. After all, he has to have a great house to offer his mate.

Left, a recent new find at BHB, this Mustache Jawfish, *Opistognathus lonchurus* is seen just beginning the dig to create it's den. They don't have hands, so they use their mouths for everything.

A pair of Seaweed Blennies, *Parablennius marmoreus* are seen here lip-locked in territorial battle. They will fight for long periods of time, then stop- pant- and then back at it again.

Call of the Wild, a Blue Throat Pike Blenny male bellows sweet nothings into the water ...that we cannot hear. Difficult to spot until they bellow. *Chaenopsis ocellata* ,very well camouflaged as thin as a pencil when at rest.

COURTSHIP & MATING BEHAVIORS

Blue Throat Pike Blennies, *Chaenopsis ocellata*, are usually seen solo. The males are more obvious when bellowing their Call of the Wild to meet their gal. Above, a female curls around a male in a really quick mating ritual or to deposit eggs. It was over in a blink of an eye.

Sailfin Blennies, *Emblemaria pandionis* (male) are one of my favorites. Here two males show off whose mouth is bigger than the other's. They never actually touch, but they will change color from deep dark blue to green to white.

DRAGONETS

Above, notice that the female Lancer's Dragonet's dorsal fin is teensy compared to the male's gynormous display sail fin. The females also display very little color change to the environment-so they are harder to detect. *Paradiplogrammus bairdi*

Lip-locking seems to be a regular thing at the BHB between males of various species struggling for territorial kingdom. In this image 2 Lancer's Dragonets duke it out for bragging rights. Notice how well camouflaged these little fellows are with their background.

COURTSHIP & MATING BEHAVIORS

Above, to get a female's attention, a male Lancer's Dragonet rapidly wiggles his tail fin and displays his sail, simultaneously, he will also begin to change color right before your eyes, as cobalt blue colors become more and more pronounced.

The final morphological result, a proud and sassy daddy-to-be male Lancer's Dragonet. From my own personal observations, the more blue a male can turn, the more successful he will be.

There are several types of flounders found at the BHB. Often you may see them chasing one another around. It's a type of courtship. If you stick around for a little while, you may see the female zip upwards releasing eggs.

Eyed Flounders, *Bothus ocellatus*

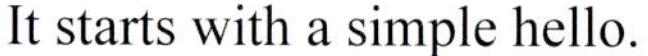

It starts with a simple hello.

Then true love is declared with a little cheek to cheek dance

COURTSHIP & MATING BEHAVIORS

I call this the lucky shot. This is a ridiculously difficult shot to get, let alone observe. Another shot that I got but wasn't great was three flounders that sandwiched themselves triple decker- mid water column spinning in opposing directions like spinning plates. Send that in if you are able to get that shot in focus.

Eyed Flounder, *Bothus ocellatus*, releasing eggs.

West Indian Fighting Conch Mating posture, *Strombus alatus*

Did you know the only time hard shell crabs can mate is when the female is molting, and is “shell-less” ? That’s her nestling under the big guy. Florida Swimming Crab, *Achelous floridanus.*

Sharpnose Puffers, *Canthigaster rostrata,* will twirl around in circles checking each other out as they spiral upwards in the water column. Their cobalt blue colors will become more vivid.

Leech Headshield slugs mating, *Chelidonura hirundinina*

Striated Frogfish, *Antennarius striatus*, mated pair, just moments before the big push. The male (the small one on the bottom), will struggle and push until he lifts his pregnant mate up into the water column for her to release her egg sac that he will then fertilize, only to watch as the little ones float away to points unknown.

A Sailfin Blenny, *Emblemaria pandionis,* flashes his sail to the world in hopes of attracting a mate.

Harlequin Pipefish, *Micrognathus ensenadae*

Dusky Jawfish *Opistognathus whitehursti* look quite similar to a Banded Jawfish, *Opistignathus macrognathus.* The Dusky Jawfish has a distinct blue to bluish black spot between the 2nd and 4th dorsal spines. At the BHB, the Banded Jawfish tend to be larger than the Dusky.

In this image, the eggs in his mouth are really quite well formed, although still have some color. The eyes look like silver bullets. There has been a lot of speculation as to the incubation period, but it is believed to be between ten and fourteen days. Mating is continual all year, however there seems to be more found around March through June. Spring fever? Perhaps.

Eggs & New Life

A Yellowhead Jawfish, *Opistognathus aurifrons,* a male incubating eggs. The males wear the pants in the family and incubate the children too. Several fish incubate their eggs in their mouths. The eggs are called a "clutch."
Fascinating to observe -especially their knack for being able to spit the eggs out, snatch a morsel of food, then suck the eggs back in, and then hide them in their gullet, as if no eggs were there at all.

Other fish that exhibit this behavior are Cardinal fish, some damsels, Banded & Dusky Jawfish, and Pipefish attach the eggs to their lower belly.

Stages of the Clutch; Banded & Dusky Jawfish

Banded Jawfish

Brand New clutch

Little color-eggs slightly opaque connecting tissue

Dusky Jawfish

Secondary stage

orange globes form, first signs of eyes and tails

Well developed, but still showing color. Eyes are fully formed and body outlines can be seen. Rumor has it that the gestation period is 10 days from the New Moon.

Eggs & New Life

Above... Almost ready- may hatch next new moon. Eggs are clearer

Close up of the eggs inside the mouth at stage 3, kind of looks like they are smiling...

Yellowline Arrow Crab with eggs.

Yellowline Arrow Crab with eggs. Up close looks like the eggs are inside a fishnet stocking. It has been observed that other Arrow crabs will attack those carrying eggs. *Stenorhynchus seticornis*

Banded Coral Shrimp with turquoise eggs, *Stenopus hispidus*

The Banded Coral Shrimp with the mint cool turquoise eggs tends to be allusive and shy. To photograph you must remain perfectly still and edge your camera up slowly in increments.

Golden Coral Shrimp with green eggs, *Stenopus scutellatus*

The Golden Coral Shrimp while carrying eggs is known to be very protective of its domain. The green eggs are carried by a thin film that holds the eggs to the belly.

Eggs & New Life

Two Spot Cardinalfish with Eggs in mouth, *Apogon pseudomaculatus*

A rare find, a Caribbean Reef octopus, *Octopus vulgaris*,with her clutch of eggs.

Lentil Sea Spider with Eggs

It never ceases to amaze me that there are spiders underwater. But this takes the cake... even they have eggs !!! The two little red things are the eyes looking at you. This is a Lentil Sea Spider... and guess what . . it is a male! This is yet another species where the male has the brooding responsibilities. Pretty cool huh? Class Pycnogonida usually hairline thin, difficult to spot. Even more incredible when you consider that prehistoric records show them to have been 12 feet tall! Thank goodness evolution decided to shrink this species down to size!

Below: Close up of a Cushion Sea Star spawning, *Oreaster reticulatus* also shot with a 10x Subsee Diopter

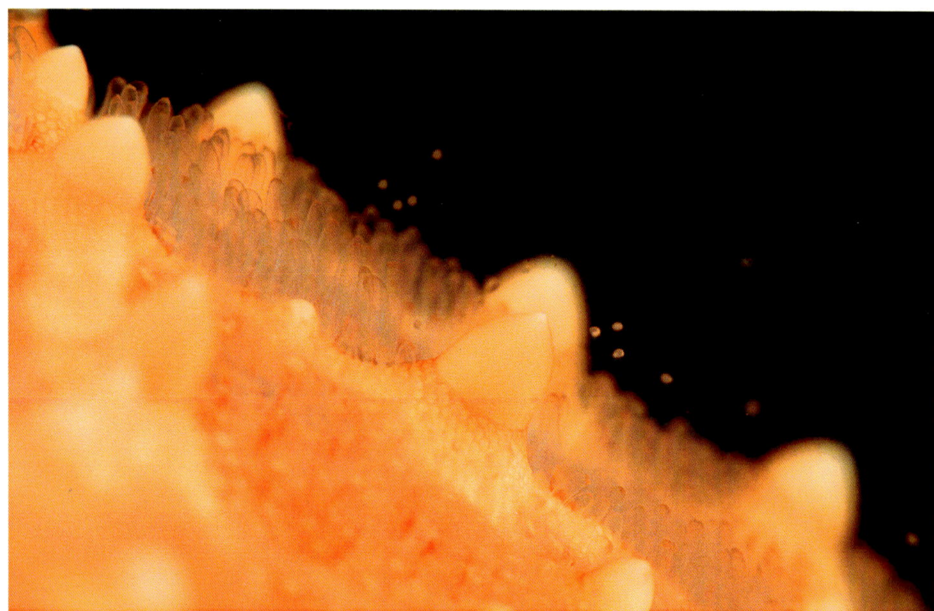

Eggs & New Life

Sergeant Major Eggs at various stages & views. **Top** (taken with a 10x Subsee Diopter) showing incredible detail of advanced stage. **Middle** Shot taken with a 105mm **Below** is what you may see by eye.

Egg Clusters

Below: In this image you can actually see the eggs coming out of the body in this particular animal's type of "ribbon strand" of eggs. Ragged Sea Hare, *Bursatella leachii* is laying its egg casing.. Follow the orange dots.

Egg Clusters

Below, Nudibranch eggs are often in circular ribbon patterns on fauna. These are the eggs of an *Oxynoe antillarum*

Couldn't help notice the facial expression as he went through early contractions. Below- a little premie pops out.

New Life Emerging

Observing a birth or soon-to-be birth is just plain exciting. This Seahorse was observed contracting, yet nothing would happen, but then, suddenly something popped out. A few more contractions, and another newbie popped out, although it did not look fully formed. The little clear piece laying out of the opening is actually the snout of one of the baby seahorses inside. Be selective when photographing this animal. Keep a fair distance when taking pictures. Use a 100-105mm so that you do not have to be right up on the animal.

Please do not over-photograph this animal. They become stressed easily and will lay down and look vacant- that's your queue to stop.

Top Left: Notice the pouch is closed, it actually clenches shut during a contraction, at which point the Seahorse's eyes seem to pop and his mouth makes that "ooh" sound. Image 2 -how many mommies remember that look on their face with the next contraction? Ruh Ro. Image 3 on the bottom, pop- a partially formed premi- pops out.

French Angelfish juvenile, *Pomacanthus paru.*

JUVENILES & THEIR PARENTS

Juvenile Gray Angelfish, *Pomacanthus arcuatus*, transitioning to adulthood

Flying gurnard dominant adult male

Juvenile female *Dactylopterus volitans*

Bandtail Sea Robin Adult

Juvenile *Prionotus Ophryas*

Scrawled Filefish Adult

Juvenile *Aluterus scriptus*

Planehead Filefish, *Monacanthus hispidus,* at various stages. Smallest being about the size of a dime. Top left is the adult

The juvenile Planehead is very similar to a Pygmy Filefish-shown above *(Stephanolepsis setifer)*.

Trunkfish

Post Larval
Juvenile

TRUNKFISH

Above : Smooth Trunkfish juveniles at different stages, *Lactophyrs triqueter*

Cowfish & Trunkfish look quite similar as juveniles

Below Trunkfish juv.

Meet "Little Man"

Above Honeycomb Cowfish Post Larval Juv. *Acanthostracion polygonia* . . . notice Cowfish juveniles have horns while trunkfish juvies do not.

COWFISH (Boxfish)

Below: Scrawled Cowfish Juvenile, *Acanthostracion quadricornis*

JUVENILES & THEIR PARENTS

Honeycomb Cowfish, *Acanthostracion polygonia*

Scrawled Cowfish are very gentle grangers of the grass and ground. *Acanthostracion quadricornis*

Caribbean Reef octopus- very curious, *Octopus vulgaris.* Be aware, they do have a beak under their cloak. If threatened can bite and cause severe pain, and bacterial infection is most harmful.

Bighead Sea Robin juvenile, *Prionotus tribulus*

OTHER JUVENILES

Baby Seaweed Blenny, *Parablennius marmoreus*

Juvenile Cushion Sea Star next to a *Chelidonura hirundinina*

Short Bigeye- juvenile, *Pristigenys alta*

Juvenile Chalk Bass, *Serranus totugarum*

Juvenile Gray Trigger fish, *Balistes capriscus*

OTHER JUVENILES

Juvenile Seahorse, *Hippocampus erectus*

Juvenile Green Razorfish, *Xyrichtys splendens*

Juvenile Gray Trigger fish, *Balistes capriscus*

Leopard Sea Robin, *Prionotus scitulus*

Juvenile Band Tail Sea Robin, *Prionotus ophryas*

Band Tail Sea Robin, *Prionotus ophryas*

Blue Spotted Sea Robin, *Prionotus roseus*

Flying Gurnard, *Dactylopterus volitans*

Smooth Trunkfish, *Lactophyrs triqueter*

Graysby, *Epinephelus cruentata*

Yellowmouth Grouper, *Mycteroperca interstitialis*

Rock Hind, *Epinephelus Adscensionis*

Red Hind, *Epinephelus guttatus*

Juvenile Smooth Trunkfish, *Lactophyrs triqueter*

Juv Honeycomb Cowfish-postlarval, *Acanthostracion polygonia*

Juv Trunkfish, *Lactophyrs trigonus*

DOTS & SPOTS

Buffalo Trunkfish, *Lactophyrs trigonus*

Scrawled Cowfish, *Acanthostracion quadricornis*
Cowfish have horns, Trunkfish do not.

Juvenile Snowy Grouper, *Epinephelus niveatus*

Spotted Eagle Ray, *Aetobatus nariniari*

Sharptail Eel, *Myrichthys breviceps*

Goldentail Moray, *Muraena milliaris*

Juvenile Blue Angelfish, *Holacanthus bermudensis*

Striped Burrfish, *Chilomeycterus schoepfi*

Cocoa Damselfish, *Stegastes planifrons*

Juvenile Seminole Goby, *Microgobius carri*

Juvenile Schoolmaster Snapper, *Lutjanus apodus*

Highhat juvenile, *Pareques acuminatus*

Spotfin Butterflyfish -juv, *Chaetodon ocellatus*

Jack Knife Fish, *Equetus lanceolatus*

The juvenile doesn't have the added colors

Blackear wrasse (term.phase), *Halichoeres poeyi*

Yellowhead Wrasse juv, *Halichoeres garnoti*

Juvenile Beaugregory, *Stegastes leucostictus*

Adults are highly decorated

Blackear wrasse (term.phase), *Halichoeres poeyi*

Spanish Hogfish juvi, *Bodianus rufus*

Barbfish (Yellow variation), *Scorpaena brasiliensis*

Green Razorfish, *Xyrichtys spendens* Male

Puddingwife Juvenile, *Halichoeres radiatus Actual size 1"*

Bluelip Parrotfish Terminal Phase, & Initial Phase, *Cryptotomus roseus*

GREEN FISH

Slippery Dick, *Halichoeres bivittatus*

Has similar colors to Green Razor, but stripes are horizontal while Razorfish has vertical stripe*s*.

Buffalo Trunkfish, *Lactophyrs trigonus*

Pygmy Filefish, *Stephanolepis setifer*

Emerald Parrotfish-Initial Phase, *Nicholsina usta*
Although blushing red colors flare up on a night dive, this Parrotfish eventually becomes a blue green color as it matures.

Spotted Goatfish, *Pseudupeneus maculatus*

Goatfish change colors. When they are actively moving about they are more white with red spots (below). But when resting they turn on the flame retardant colors- to spook off evil predators while they snooze!

Spotted Goatfish, *Pseudupeneus maculatus*

This Goatfish is seen in his dining attire (active phase coloring)

Frogfish, a fish with feet, come in a variety of colors, patterns and textures. This brilliant red fellow was a rare find and is not a usual suspect at the BHB.

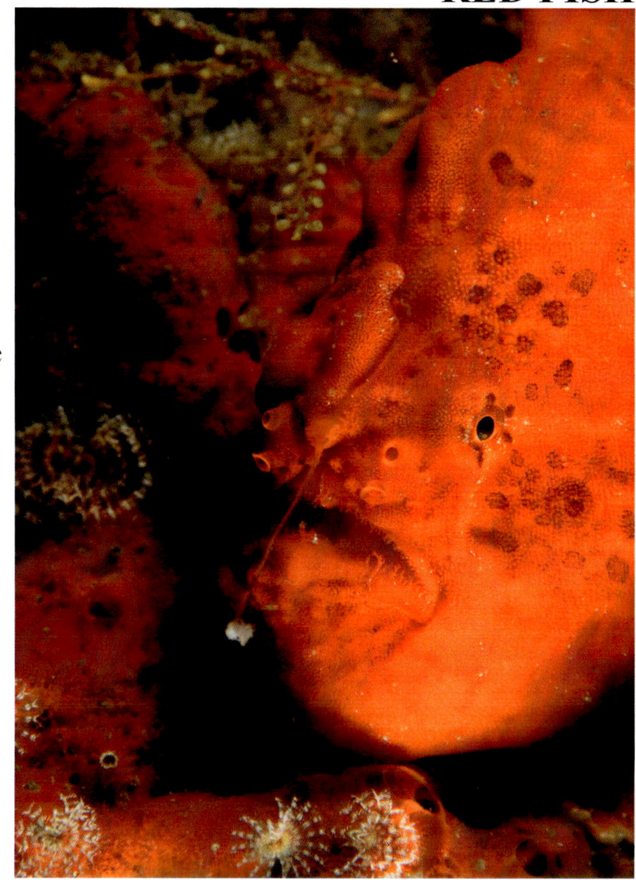

Longlure Frogfish, Red, *Antennarius multiocellatus*

The Barbfish looks like a really really red or mustard yellow scorpion fish- but with webbed necking ... of alien ancestry for sure.

Barbfish, *Scorpaena brasiliensis*

Blue Chromis are rarely found at the BHB. Found on the north side of the little bridge by the wreck

Blue Chromis, *Chromis cyanea*

MidnightBlue Parrotfish, *Scarus coelestinus*

These beauties seem to be growing in numbers over on the west side. It seems only appropriate that the only in-focus shot I could get was on a night dive. Parrotfish at the Bridge are aloof to divers and seem to go out of their way to avoid eye contact.

Peacock Flounder, *Bothus lunatus* This highly decorated soldier is wearing his mating colors.

Cocoa Damselfish juvenile, *Stegastes variabilis* This is how they eat- just open mouth & let particles fly in with the moving current.

DANGEROUS SEA LIFE

Green Moray Eel, *Gymnothorax funebris*

Consider aggressive, but they are nearsighted, if you keep some distance, you can get relatively close for photos, but approach with caution. Some are free swimmers, meaning they will advance without warning, ready to strike.

Besides the nasty fangs, the more likely danger from a bite is the bacteria within that can cause a terrible infection. Each type of eel has its own traits towards aggressiveness. For instance the Spotted Moray while considered aggressive, is usually more likely to give up and duck into a hole.

Spotted Moray Eel, *Gymnothorax moringa*

Usually quite timid at the bridge. More interested in foraging for something to eat, and even look cute, but be wary of those fangs. Never get hands too close. The fangs are stacked behind one another to secure prey in a locked jaw.

Spotted Moray; *Gymnothorax moringa*

EELS

Spotted Spoon Nosed Eel, *Echiophis intertinctus* -emerges from the sand at dusk. Very prehistoric looking, wouldn't you say?

Sharptail Eel, *Myrichthys breviceps*

Goldspot Eel, *Myrichthys ocellatus*

Neither of these are considered aggressive eels.

EELS

Goldentail Eel, *Muraena miliaris* Notice the variations in color. They will darken and brighten their colors prompted by various emotions or threats.

Both are Purplemouth Morays

Purplemouth Moray, *Gymnothorax vicinis*

The Whip Eel, *Bascanichthys scuticarus* has lovingly become known as the Jimmy Durante Eel, due to its bulbous rostrum. The first time we found it, we were told that there existed no pictures of a live specimen. Rarely seen alive, it is a prize shot to add to your collection- or even just to see one. Extremely timid. Do not approach quickly or it will recede into its den and not come back until you have gone. Highly effected by shadow and current impression. Found in isolated sand stretches along the edge closest to the channel.

DANGEROUS SEA LIFE

Not so Dangerous EELS

Brown Garden Eel, *Heteroconger longissimus*

Yellow Garden Eel, *Heteroconger luteolus*

If you find yourself needing a photographic challenge, hunker down along the perimeter of the Garden eels found at the bend on the East side, and try getting as close as possible for a cool shot. Warning, it takes a lot of patience.

Things That Sting

Red Tipped Fireworm, *Chloeia viridis*

#1 on the hit parade at Blue Heron Bridge is most definitely the massive numbers of Fireworms. They are everywhere. Amply named, their bristles impose a firey pain unlike any other. Their quills can be found embedded in the faces of Seaweed Blennies, juvenile scorpionfish, and many photographers gloves. It is not known if the Blennies like to eat them or attack the fireworms.

An unlucky juvenile scorpionfish lies still, paralyzed, showing tell tale signs of having done battle with a fireworm.

The Multifarious Life of a Fireworm

Victim of the Quills

This poor Seaweed blenny appears to have turned blue in severe pain, fireworm quills bearding his chin.

These small creatures range in size from that of a small caterpillar up to 10 inches long, and are fearsome predators with a voracious appetite. They may look cute and fuzzy- but don't even think about it.

Their quills are hollow, containing a highly toxic neurotoxin rendered to the victim via nematocysts that they use to take down prey and render it paralyzed. If you don't believe this ... check out the next few pages!

(Above) This Red Tipped has inflated its pharynx out and down and is inhaling the sandy bottom searching for food.

The venom filled bristles shoot out perhaps hundreds of microscopic poison filled nematocysts. Nematocysts contain a firing mechanism, much like a harpoon with a barb at the end. The barb only moves one way . . . inward. Attempts to brush it off, simply break off leaving the barb and microscopic sac in tact in the skin of the victim, free to continue deeper... and not all nematocysts completely fire upon impact. This can prolong the effects of the toxin being delivered continuously over long periods of time.

What is a nematocyst? Can I see it?

Nope, you can't see it, but you sure can feel it. Once a nematocyst barb has buried into your skin, its sole purpose is to deliver the microscopic toxin. To the touch, your skin feels as if it has millions of splinters in it. To press on them with anything is torture, and will most likely push the rest of the quills along with their stinging toxins into your skin. The key to relief is to negate the toxin with enzymes. First gently rinse with fresh water to rinse away loose bristles. Vinegar or even your own urine are the most helpful topical solutions, as the enzymes are capable of temporarily neutralizing the toxin. However, hot water- the hottest you can stand, is helpful to force the nematocysts to fire/explode, releasing the toxin. This is done to reduce continuous prolonged firey eruptions of your skin from weeks to days. The blisters are painful, you may become fevered. If the area affected becomes inflamed and swollen, see a doctor and quickly if it becomes horrific within minutes or hours, as you may be susceptible to the toxin.

DANGEROUS SEA LIFE

Fireworms will stand up and sniff about seeking prey. Anything swimming by that accidentally touches the fine setae can set off the nematocyst triggers.

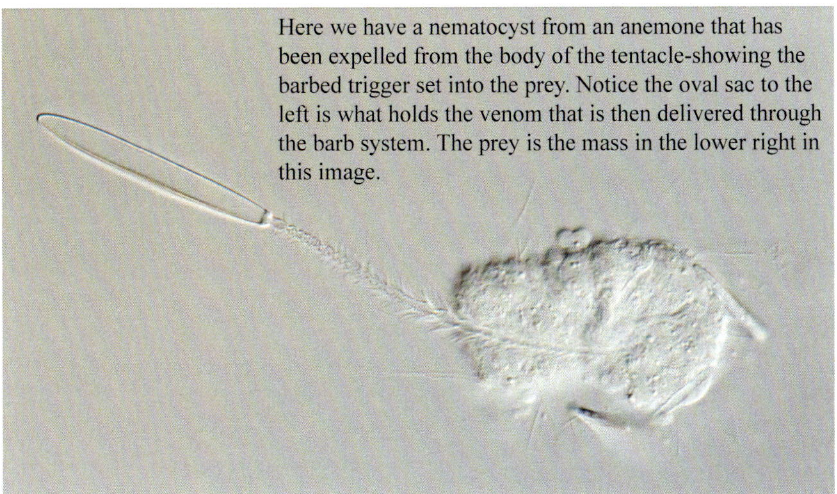

Here we have a nematocyst from an anemone that has been expelled from the body of the tentacle-showing the barbed trigger set into the prey. Notice the oval sac to the left is what holds the venom that is then delivered through the barb system. The prey is the mass in the lower right in this image.

Photographed by Waldo Nell with a microscope using DIC for illumination - nematocysts are pretty much translucent -this is one method of making them visible. (Above) The Aiptasia nematocysts are about 13µm long. That is VERY tiny. A human red blood cell is about 7µm in diameter as comparison. µm is micrometer measurement. 13 µm comparable to 1 acrylic fiber.

They've been observed stunning a fish swimming by in a school that got too close, only to be immediately taken down and eaten alive. Bearded Fireworm, Hermodice carunculata

Can taste test through "hydraulic mining" technique with its tongue

Another variation of the black lined fireworm

Able to consume things larger than itself

Coughs it up when it doesn't taste good & did I mention... it has a tongue!

If you happen upon a flurry of these creatures, it is likely a dead or dying animal is nearby or, if close to a full or new moon, they are beginning to gather together for a spawning about to occur. Time to leave the water.

From above, while cruising around for something to photograph, we witnessed hundreds of fireworms all heading in one direction, like fans swarming into a coliseum. What we found was unbelievable. A full grown octopus was being taken down by fireworms. It was still alive, and couldn't seem to escape the death grips. As well, that many fireworms, the toxins had paralyzed it.

Our best guess was that perhaps this octopus was a female who's eggs had matured, and was dying already. What an awful way to go.

Once fully engorged, one fireworm receded, revealing its path of destruction. It had completely stripped the octopus's tentacle of its suction cups and skin. If you've ever tried to eat octopus, you know how tough the meat is... which should give you a good idea of the strength of the fireworm.

Fireworms also forage for food upon live Bubble Shells, *Haminoea succinea*. The purply color is believed to be a chemical release from the live Bubble shell to ward off its attacker.

Another favorite food is sipping jellyfish juice. Also note that many stinging creatures eat other stinging creatures.

Above Bearded Fireworm, *Hermodice carunculata*

Blackline Fireworm, *Chloeia viridis*

DANGEROUS SEA LIFE

Parts of the Fireworm

Close up of the Beauty and the Beast all-in-one.

- The *setae* are the bunched up white bristles sticking out of the parapodia, which can retract and puff up if disturbed or attacked. These contain the nematocysts.

- The ornate orange frill segments are the gill filaments.

- The orange bonnet is the *"caruncle"* and is believed to contain its sensory functions.

- The Rhino horns on the prostomium are the worm's *median antenna.*

Below you can clearly see the exposed *pharynx* (red mouth) tempted into a taste test of a fish fin that gets too close.

Reproduction

Near to a full moon, fireworms will appear to become quite chummy, while normally leading a solo life except at shared meals.

To the right, males flash lights throughout their heads and bonnet is a giveaway that there is to be a celebration tonight ... meaning in Fireworm tongue, "Meet me at the surface tonight!"

Opposite page left; in this image you can see their double eyes not always visible. The illuminated speckles are a show of amorous mood swings.

At dusk near a full moon, hundreds of fireworms emerge from beneath the sand, a short caressing, and then they ascend to the surface of the water column in the shallows, close to shore. A change occurs.
Females emit a phosphorescent greenish glow. Males flash tiny lights! (albeit not visible by our eyes). They then swim to the surface to procreate.

Greenish *glow*

CNIDARIANS

JELLYFISH

Pink Meanie, *Drymonema larsoni* found in February- a rare sighting as is normally an ocean traveler Highly toxic

Jelly Hydromedusa, *Aequorea forskalea* . . 8 eyes of the jellyfish look like lights along the top dome. Mildly toxic

Club Hydromedusa, *Orchistoma pileus*

Portuguese Man-O-War, *Physalia physalis* Highly toxic

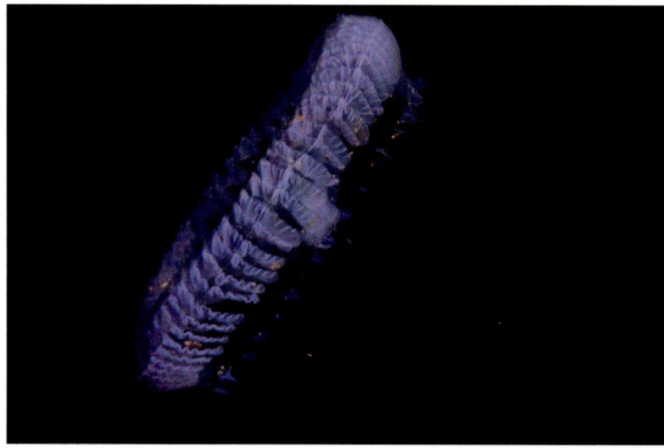

Many-Ribbed *Aequorea aequorea, Hydromedusae Aequorea sp.*is related to this jellyfish.

Warty Anemone, *Pelagia notiluca on the hunt*

above, A juvenile version of the *Pelagia notiluca* . . . size of golf ball

Apparently this group are seen traveling together in mass aggregations on either side of the Atlantic Ocean between January and March. The *Pelagia notiluca, Aequorea forskalea* and the Portuguese Man-O-War are a tighter trio. Highly toxic

Warty Anemone, *Pelagia notiluca relaxed*

CNIDARIANS

(Right) undescribed 8 eyed jellyfish.

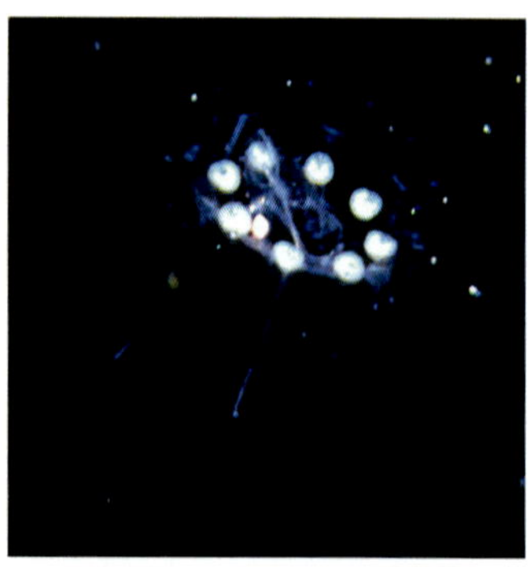

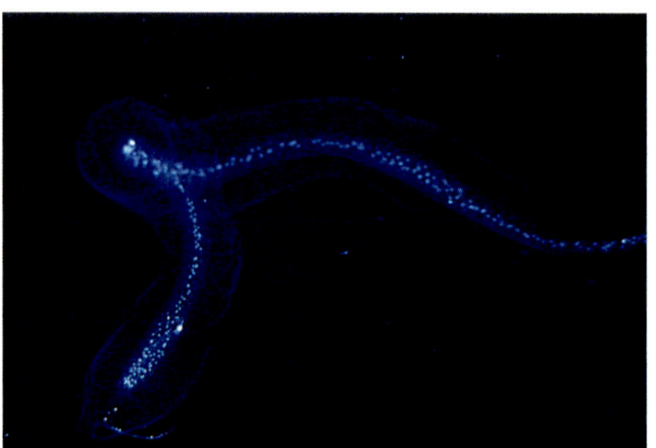

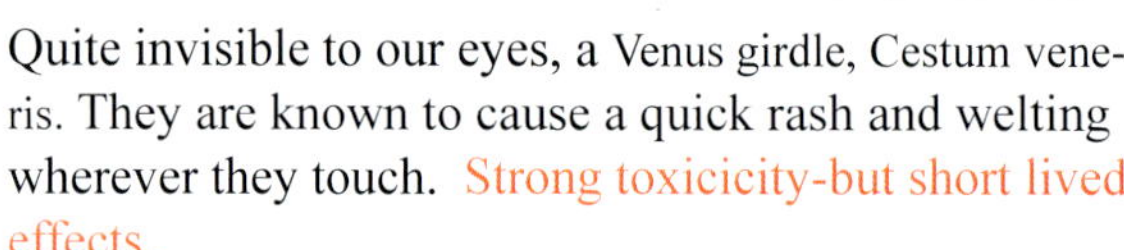

Quite invisible to our eyes, a Venus girdle, Cestum veneris. They are known to cause a quick rash and welting wherever they touch. Strong toxicicity-but short lived effects.

(Right) *Hydromedusa liriope* a stalked jellyfish.

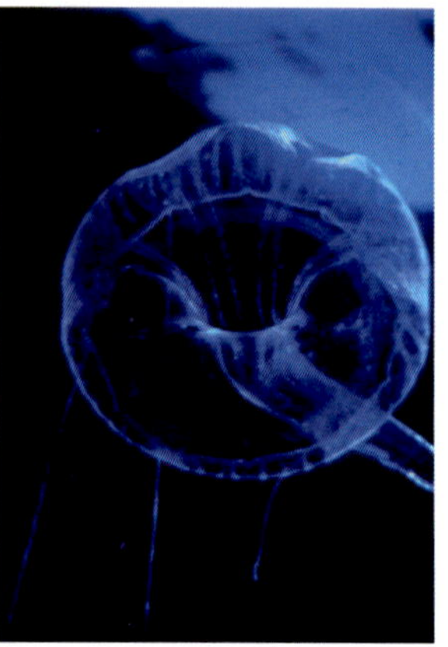

Cnidarians is the Phylum that contains Jellyfish, (Anthozoa) Corals, Anemones, Cubuzoa (box jellyfish) Sea pens, Hydrozoans, and Staurozoa (stalked jellyfish).

They are carnivorous animals. They contain nematocyst cells, which is a stinging structure made up of a hollow thread that has barbs inside and a hairlike trigger outside. This trigger is called a Cnidocyte. Once activated it thrusts outward-turning itself inside out--stabbing the prey and delivering the poisonous toxin. The root word from Greek is cnidaria meaning nettle.

True Jellyfish belong to the Class Scyphozoa; examples include Moon Jellies, Mediterranean Jellyfish, Sea Nettles, Blue Jellies, and Lion's Mane Jellyfish, deemed one of the most toxic in the world.

The Class Cubuzoa is referred to as Box Jellyfish- which includes the deadly box jelly of Australia and it's cousin in the Atlantic and Caribbean, the Sea Wasp.

The Class Hydrozoa includes Hydromedusal jellyfish, Siphonophores, anemones and corals, all possessing nematocysts. Includes Portuguese Man-Of-War.

The Class Staurozoa (stalked jellyfish) -they do not alternate between a polyp and medusal stage. Most have trumpet shaped bodies with a stalk and tentacles.

Upsidedown Jellyfish vs Mangrove Upsidedown Jellyfish. Yes there are 2 kinds. The Mangrove kind (right) -most often found at BHB has the leafy blue plumes. *Cassiopea xamachana.* Also does not pose a huge threat with regards to stinging power.

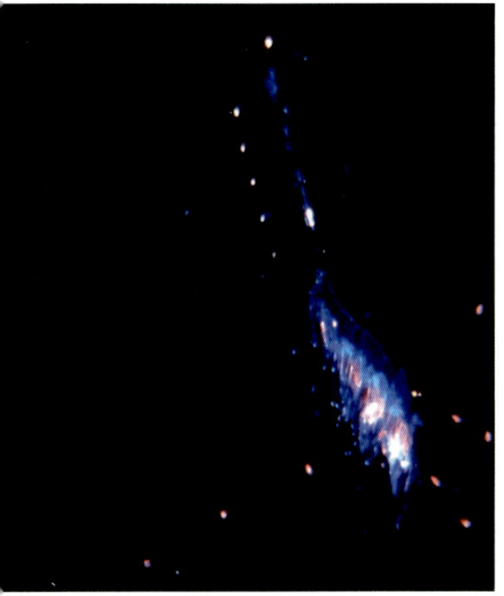

Peared-Bell Siphonophore, *Agalma okeni* Strong toxicicity- but short lived effects -will cause welts that dissipate in an hour or 2.

Undescribed jellyfish Highly toxic

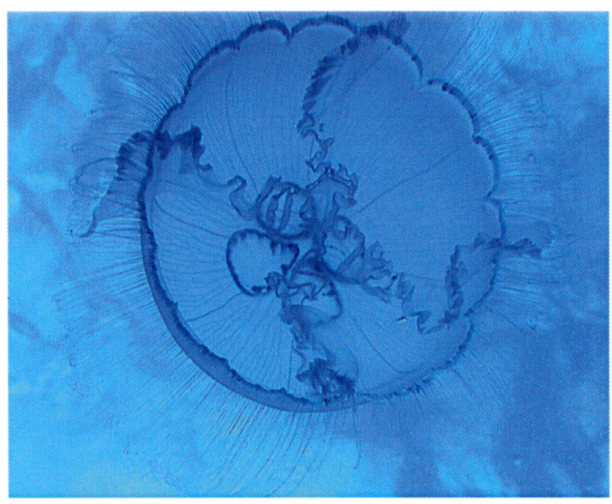

Phases of a Moon Jellyfish, *Aurelia aurita.* (above) mid August full grown

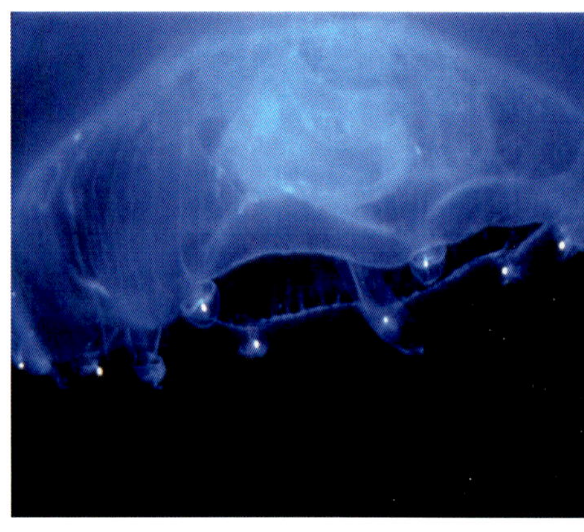

They eyes of the Jellyfish (8 in total) are visible in this image.

In late October, Moon Jellies approximately 9" in diameter that look like this are females, about to release their eggs to fertilize them with collected spermatazoa from the males.

The males release their spermatazoa in the morning. The water column becomes full of white cat hair like particles, that the females take command of enveloping them within their dome. The propagation is an all day affair, making the waters nearly intolerable due to the high concentration of free flowing nematocysts. After fertilization has occurred the females pulsate in a twisting motion like a washing machine cycle, only to tear off and drop their "skirt." The nematocysts seem to be particularly potent during propagation.

Otherwise normally, the Moon Jellies are not considered to be that toxic. In fact it is possible to touch them without being stung or barely being stung. The female has 4 distinct gonads (pink or violet), while the male's are yellowish brown.

Flattened Helmet Comb Jelly, *Beroe ovata*

Brown-Spotted Comb Jelly, *Leucothea pulchra*

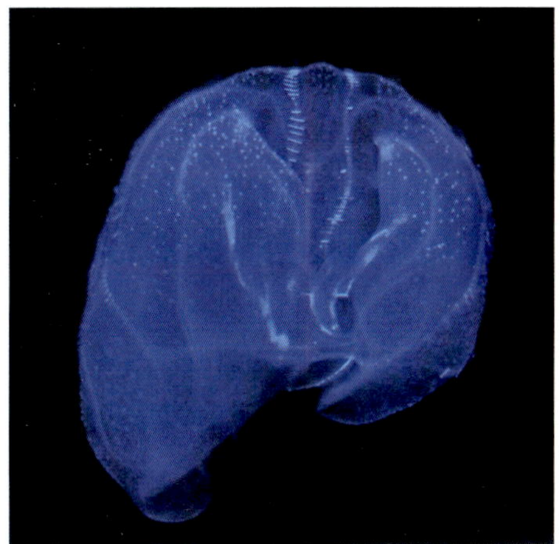

Sea Walnut, *Mnemiopsis mccradyi*

Spot Winged Comb Jelly, *Ocyropsis sp.*

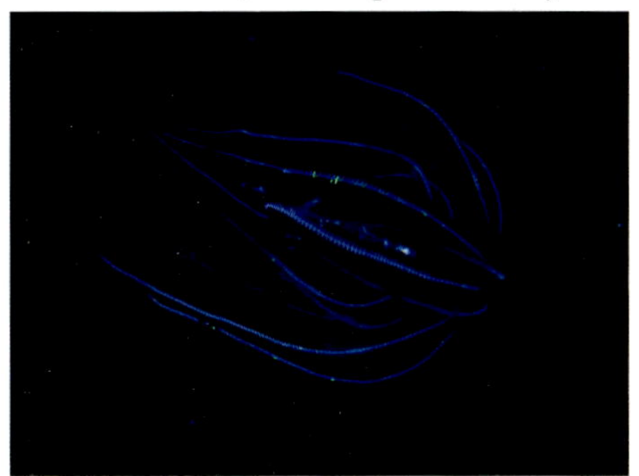

Warty Comb Jelly, *Leucothea multicornis*

Brown-Spotted Comb Jelly opening to feed

HYDROIDS

Hydroids contain nematocyst stinging cells. They belong to the family Hydrozoa, which includes Anemones and Jellyfish. Brushing up against them can cause burning blisters and rash up to 1 week

Touch-me not Sponge with feather hydroids. *Neofibularia nolatangiegere*. Often 2 types of stinging creatures will reside together. In this case this sponge packs a punch.

Pink mouth hydroid - *Ectopleura marina* a favorite dining place for nudibranchs

Pink mouth hydroid - *Ectopleura marina Home to pink Skeleton Shrimp*

Unbranched Hydroid, *Thyroscyphus marginatus*

Branching Hydroid, *Sertularella diaphana on Red Fire Sponge. Both pack a punch*
Highly toxic

Algae hydroid, Thyroscyphus ramosus, a favorite for nudibranchs and fireworms
Highly toxic

White Stinger, *Macrorchynchia philippina*. A favorite hideaway for Skeleton Shrimps and Clear shrimp

White Stinger, *Macrorchynchia philippina.* A favorite hideaway for Skeleton Shrimps and Clear shrimp - Closeup

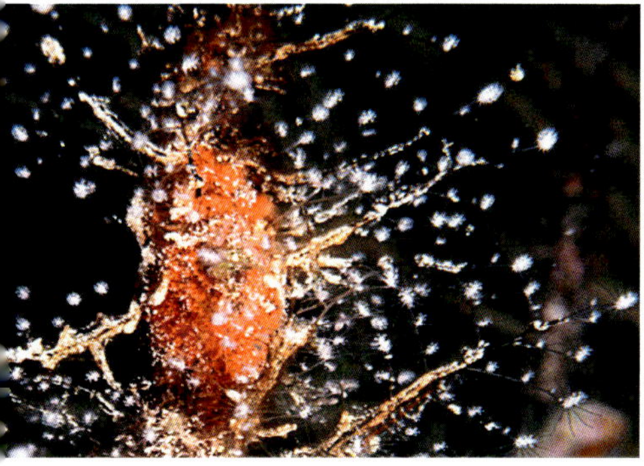

Christmas Tree Hydroid, *Pennaria disticha*

Club Hydroids, *Clava leptostyla*

Unbranched Hydroid, *Thyroscyphus marginatus*

Algae hydroid, *Thyroscyphus ramosus,* also acts as a protective barrier for small residents against predators.

ANEMONES

Although Anemones look like plants, they too are Cnidarians, which means carnivorous animal. They also carry nematocysts, and are capable of causing severe blistering and numbness if handled.

Transparent Tube Dwelling Anemone, undetermined

Hitchhiking Anemone, *Calliactis tricolor* Usually found attached to large hermit crabs.

Banded Tube Dwelling Anemone, *Isarachnanthus nocturnus*

Banded Tube Dwelling Anemone, *Isarachnanthus nocturnus*

Banded Tube Dwelling Anemone, *Isarachnanthus nocturnus*

Turtle Grass Anemone, *Viatrix globulifera*

Hitchhiking Anemone, *Calliactis tricolor*

ANEMONES

Lined Tube Dwelling Anemone, *undescribed*

Here you have a sand anemone eating a Portuguese Man-O-War ? Highly toxic

Corkscrew Anemone, *Bartholomean annulata*
Mild (home to the Pederson Cleaner Shrimp)

Lined Tube Dwelling Anemone

Branching Anemone, *Lebrunia danae*

Wispy Tube Dwelling Anemone, *Undescribed*

Berried Anemone, *Alicia mirabilis*

Giant Tube Dwelling Anemone; *Ceriantheormorphe brasiliensis*

Berried Anemone, *Alicia mirabilis*

Berried Anemone, *Alicia mirabilis*

ELECTROGENIC FISH

STARGAZER

Southern Stargazer, *Astrodcopus y-graecum* Extremely difficult to distinguish difference between Southern & a Northern Stargazer. Nestles itself in the rubble. You may only see a few polka dots when diving and looking down. Can deliver an electric shock from behind the eyes up to 50 watts. Do not get your face too close to them as electric current travels through

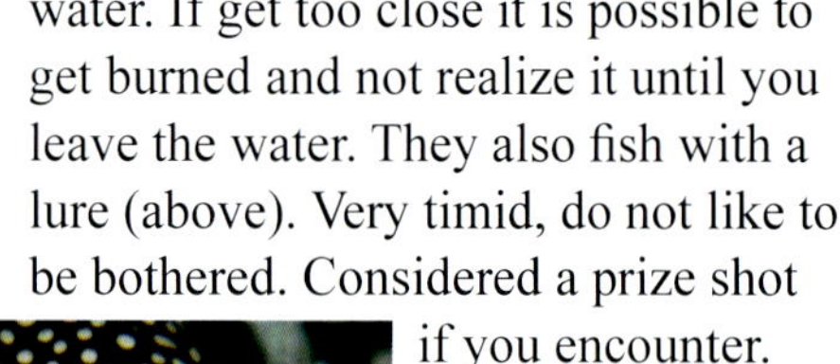

water. If get too close it is possible to get burned and not realize it until you leave the water. They also fish with a lure (above). Very timid, do not like to be bothered. Considered a prize shot if you encounter. They range in size from something that would fit in the palm of your hand to 2 feet long. Buries itself in the sand. Submerged body usually 3 times larger than part revealed.

ELECTRIC RAY

Rarely seen at the BHB, the Lesser Electric Ray, *Narcinine bancroftii,* sometimes referred to as a Torpedo Ray, grows to about 18" long. It is a pinkish gray-brown color, with brown splotches. Tail has 2 dorsal fins.

Also has two electric organs, elongated in shape, running from the front of the eyes. The electric organs used for stunning prey and warding of predators, capable of electrocution at 14-37 volts.

PREDATORS
With POISONOUS SPINES

Cownose Rays, *Rhinoptera javanica* This school has been witnessed a few times at the bridge around October.

As graceful as they are, the danger with rays is the poisonous spines at the base of the tail (closest to the body). They can have 1 to 5 spines depending on the species. The toxin can take a grown man to his knees, and is seriously painful. Rays will settle to the sand and cover themselves to rest. While camouflaged, one can easily step on one while entering a sandy beach area, or a photographer may settle to the sand for a photograph unaware of the animal under sand, when the tail can whip upwards and strike the poisonous spine into the flesh. Be aware of your landing zone for any camouflaged denizens of the deep.

Although the **Spotted Eagle Rays,** *Aetobatus narinari* **(right)** tend to always be on the move, they do forage for food through the sand and may come close, so be aware of their proximity and don't try to grab their tail. Normally they live by the "5 foot-safe-distance-to-humans policy."

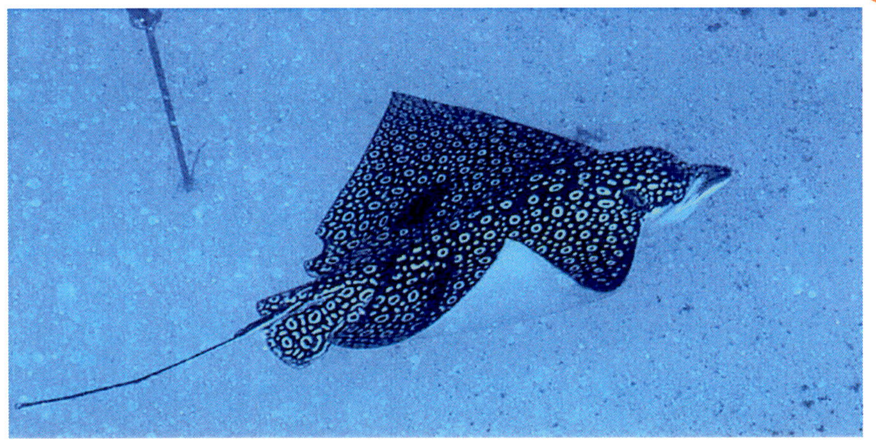

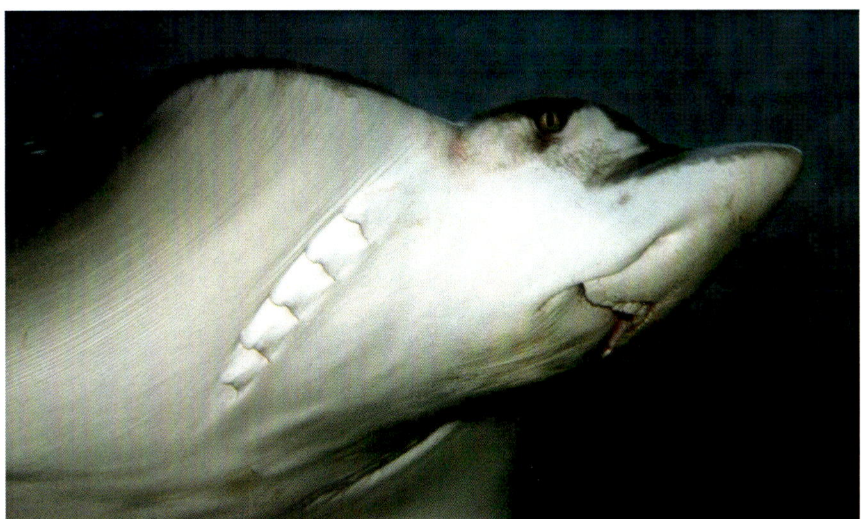

PREDATORS
With POISONOUS SPINES

RAYS

Butterfly ray, *Gymnura micrura*

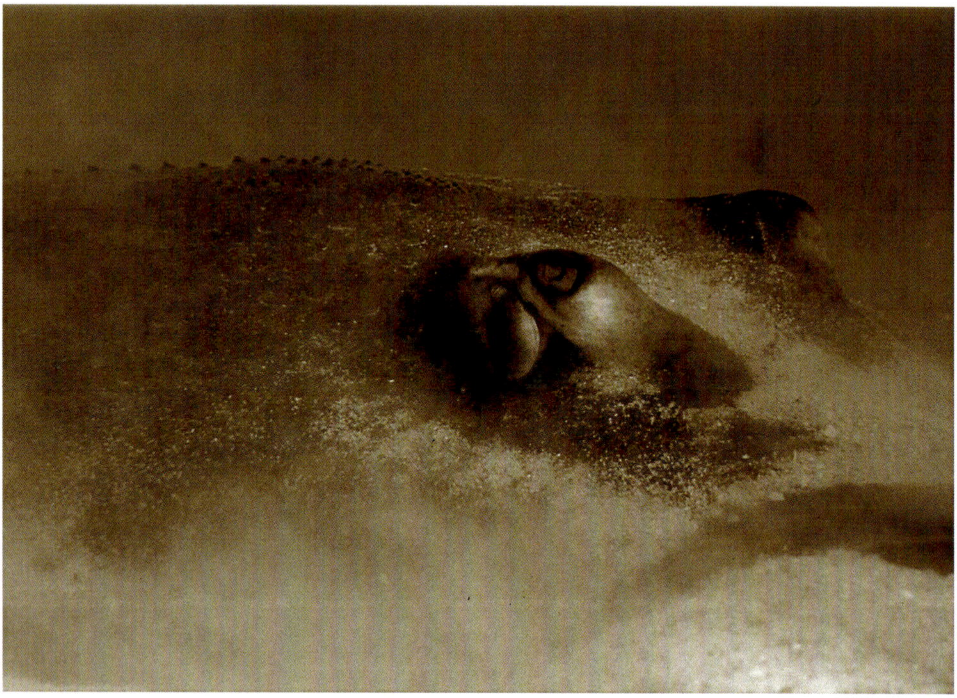

Roughtail stingray in the murk, *Dasyatis centroura*

Butterfly ray, *Gymnura micrura*

Southern Stingray, *Dasyatis americana*

Yellow Stingray, *Urolphus jamaicensis*

Yellow Stingray, *Urolophus jamaicensis*

Here is a close up of the spine to avoid. Unfortunately, Yellow Stingrays account for the majority of the stings in shallow waters and beach entries. They love to bury themselves with a fine layer of sand to camouflage themselves.

SPINES THAT STING

Lionfish, *Pterois volitans*

Yes, the invasion of the Lionfish has found its way into the Blue Heron Bridge area. Several have been captured, usually as juveniles. Rarely see full grown at the Bridge.

Not only do the dorsal fins contain a highly potent toxin, but there are Anal fins that are venomous, as well as a pelvic fin spine, down by the front first fin. There are usually 8 spines across the top-with the 8th one being quite short and almost hidden. To be stung can cause serious ill effects, besides the localized pain, may include nausea and vomiting for several hours.

PREDATORS
With POISONOUS SPINES

Red Barbfish, *Scorpaena brasiliensis*

Yellow Barbfish, *Scorpaena brasiliensis*

Red Barbfish, *Scorpaena brasiliensis*

Reef Scorpionfish, *Scorpaena caribbaeus*

Red Barbfish, *Scorpaena brasiliensis*

Reef Scorpionfish, *close up of the dorsal fins that contain the spines*

Scorpionfish, Barbfish, Lionfish all carry poisonous spines in their dorsal fins. They blend in well with their surroundings most often.

Balloonfish, *Diodon holocanthus* only inflate when molested as a diversion tactic to evade predators. Their spines are not filled with toxins like the others on the page, but carry bad bacteria. Their skin is poisonous if eaten.

The biggest problem occurs when divers inadvertently rest their hand on the spines of a camouflaged dorsal fin.

Recently the Lionfish have made their way to the BHB and most injuries occur due to mishandling while trying to capture and remove them. Taking a class is recommended to learn how to handle without getting stung. The venom in the spines is harrowing.

OTHER STINGING THINGS

Long Spined Urchin; *Echinometra lucunter*

Variegated Urchin, *Lytechinus variegatus* come in a variety of colors. Favorite home for the cute little Bumblebee shrimp

Purple Urchin, *Arbacia punctulata*

Great Barracuda, *Sphyraena barracuda*
Although they can show a great set of fangs, and can appear very menacing at times, they seem content to just "patrol" the area. Warning, they are attracted to sparkly things, so . . . hide your jewelry!

(below) Houndfish, *Tylosurus crocodilus*. Most needlefish seem to also keep the 5 foot safe-distance-to humans rule when it comes to divers. However, take a look at those choppers. Is this prehistoric looking enough for you? These are not the teeth of a vegetarian.

Nurse Shark, *Ginglymostoma cirratum* Quite rare to see, but seen a number of times at Blue Heron Bridge.

Bull Shark, *Carcharhinus leucas*. Definitely a rare sighting, last time seen was over 8 years ago. This was photographed on a night dive at the Bridge, when we got turned around and were hedging out toward the Channel by mistake. This was shot on film with a 35mm lens with a Nikonos V. I managed one shot as a "proof of life." Bull sharks are known to be adventurous, and have been recorded swimming up rivers, however, seriously don't need to be concerned about running into one. Folks have also questioned nurse sharks present at the BHB too, until everyone sees one there. It's the ocean. Everything moves about.

Web Burrfish; *Chilomycterus antillarum*

Scaly-Tailed Mantis Shrimp, *Lysiosquilla scabricauda* Clearing out it's burrow

BIZARRE & UNUSUAL

Striped Burrfish; *Chilomycterus schoepfi*

Detail of the eyes of a Mantis...pupils appear to rotate around the oblong globe

Spottedfin Tonguefish; *Symphurus diomedianus*

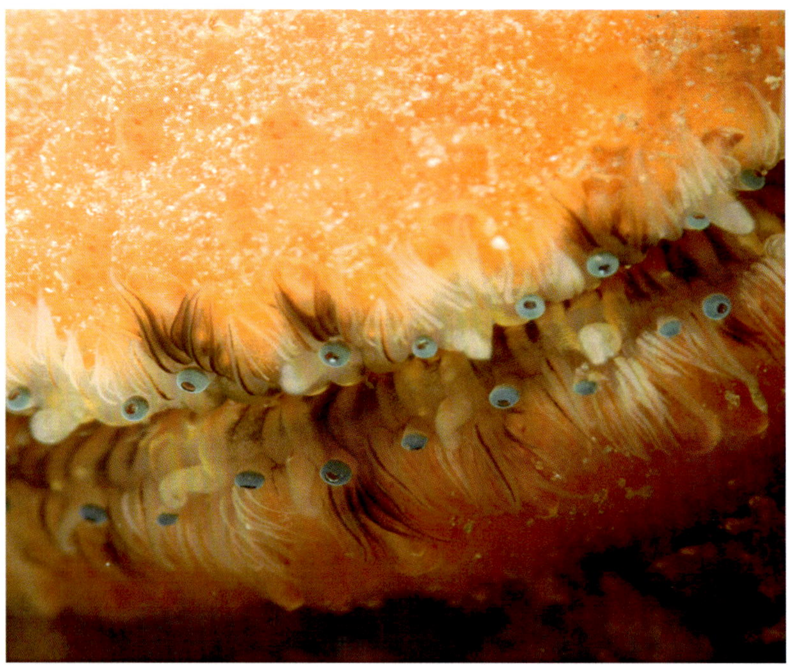

Did you know that scallops have lots and lots of eyes?

BIZARRE & UNUSUAL

You are not seeing double. This is a molting Arrow Crab. As they grow, crabs must molt like a snake, they shed their outer shell. Amazing they can get out all in one piece . . . even the legs.

Sea Pansy, *Renilla reniformis* Actually a type of soft coral and is actually a colony made up of multiple organisms. Known to appear after N'or easters, it is also a Cnidarian, related to Jellyfish!

Have you ever seen a lobster eat a fish? Caribbean Spiny Lobster, *Panulirus argus*

BIZARRE & UNUSUAL

Ornate Scale Worm, *Polychaete* Worm.

Bobbitt Worms, *Eunice sp.* They are very timid, don't like too much light, better photographed with a red filter, and commonly seen at night or dark cloudy days.

CAMOUFLAGE

Spongy Decorator Crab, *Macrocoeloma trispinosum*

Decorator Crabs come in all shapes and sizes. They are the kings and queens of camouflage and disguise. Second only to perhaps the sneaky Mimic Octopus. They adorn themselves with sponge, polyps, algae, whatever is around. But if you look closely they have some very unique dressings and very specific attitudes. I call them the Punk Rockers of the BHB. On any given night dive, the place comes alive with the down town scene, in some locations close to the pilings or even specific areas on the pilings. They seem to take pride in their "apparel." Sometimes several will appear together checking out each other's body art. Really a lot of fun to observe.

(Right Page bottom left) Southern Tear Drop Crab, *Pelia rotunda*

CAMOUFLAGE

Even Frogfish adapt to their surroundings and change their color at will. The Frogfish pair that look quite brown are Striated Frogfish, suddenly muted their colors, to blend in with their surroundings, which I've never seen occur before. Like Scorpionfish, they use the camouflage for hunting purposes and most likely to escape predation as well.

An Atlantic Long Armed Octopus, *Macroptritopus defilippi*, - aka what the locals refer to as the Mimic Octopus, mimics the sandy bottom colors and textures, hoping to blend in with it's surroundings for a stealthy sneak attack upon a nearby flounder.

How They Hide

Seahorses at the Bridge will find a sponge to blend in with, while Frilled Seahorses are likely to find refuge in hairy hydroids.

As it turns out, most fish have the ability to change color, and adapt to their surroundings. Camouflage is a means of survival in the underwater world. But as you get to know your subjects, you adapt your eyes to the surroundings, keeping a sharp look out for eyes hidden in the foliage. Keep a keen eye out for movement, ever so slight to be the tip off to life in the weeds. Get familiar with your subject's favorite food. As stated in the beginning of the book, if you know what to look for, you will find it. And so becomes the most thrilling part of the underwater photographer's journey... the find.

Seahorses for instance, although all *Hippocampus erectus* at the bridge, come in a variety of colors and frill and fringe. The trained eye tends to find seahorses all the time, while others have to just be lucky and hope one jumps out in front of them or hope its a brilliant bright orange color. They like to tuck into surroundings of the same color, or perhaps they change to the color of the surrounding. I've only witnessed them darken and lighten.

Scorpionfish blend into their surroundings so well, that if it were not for their eyes they would be invisible.

Octopii will go 3-D to blend in with their surroundings.

A Checkered Pufferfish, *Sphoeroides testudineus,* uses the rubble as its Picasso background.

When photographing macro, search the hydroids. They are a good source of study and amazing examples of camouflage. This clear shrimp probably took three dives, before I could get it in focus. I kept seeing ghostly movement out of the corners of my eyes.

A Yellow Stingray has buried itself under the rubble, using that as it's camouflage. Always be aware of your surroundings and what creatures lurk beneath the rubble.

Striated Frogfish, *Antennarius striatus* waves it's split lure hoping to coax out some live lunch.

The Frogfish actually goes "fishing with it's lure. If you spy a worm twirling about in mid water- home in on that- as it is most likely the lure of a frogfish. And each Frogfish has it's own style and it's own type of lure!

The purpose.. if a little fish goes for the lure, they fling it back & open their large mouth and suck it down in a NY second.

FISH WITH LURES & FEET

Most folks do not think of fish as having feet, or walking along the sandy bottoms. It is such an unusual occurrence, it takes most by surprise their first time witnessing this behavior. The BHB is one of the few places that you can see this almost all the time.

While the lure looks like a single fluffy thing (upper left page) - it actually splits open and can be twirled like a twizzle stick by the frogfish.

Polka Dot Batfish, *Ogcocephalus radiatus*

The lure system is a little bit different than the Frogfish, but the idea is still the same. The Polka Dotted batfish here, will stnad completely still, using its colorations to blend into it's surroundings. The Probiscus, or lure flaps open and shut almost looking like Fred Flintstone snapping his fingers to an inaudible beat. The lure is much short- but they too can suck up half the ocean if need be for a meal that takes the bate.

Photo Tip: Batfish are slow moving, and hold still for long periods of time, and may not feel like much of a photo challenge, right? Wrong. They are very sensitive to movement. The closer you get, the more they will move their face away from yours. The key is to not make eye contact as that seems to be an admission that you are up to no good. If you do not move, find a place that you can gradually ease your camera up to them slowly- they may drop that lure for you to get the photograph.

Shortnose Batfish, *Ogcocephalus nasutus*

Photo Tip: When photographing fish that are red, it is necessary to shoot darker, as there seems to be a sheen on their coating- that can really blast the reds right back at you. Or you can move your strobes out a little to compensate and not accidentally highlight that red.

Flying Gurnard, *Dactylopterus volitans*

Sailfin Blenny, *Emblemarius pandionis*

Leopard Searobin, *Prionotus scitulus*

These are some of the more prized critters to be on the lookout for; ***Upper left & top right;*** the Flying Gurnard.

Left middle: Sailfin Blenny & Leopard Sea Robin juvenile

Lower, Male Lancer's Dragonet displays his beautiful dorsal fin.

Lower Right: Blue Throat Pike Blenny displaying (mating behavior).

Flying Gurnard, *Dactylopterus volitans*

Blue Throat Pike Blenny, *Chaenopsis ocellata*

Using a Reefnet 10x Diopter, combined with a 105mm lens, we are able to see better close ups of animals, with detail not readily seen with the bare eye.
I have spent hours exploring a single clump, just to see, what I normally wouldn't see by eye. It is truly fascinating, each layer that we can uncover. This chapter is devoted to showing you some of the possibilities.

On a particularly mucky day, I found a small pocket of clearer water by a rock where little specs were moving about -equidistant to themselves, and having no clue what they were, my best guess was that they were newborn fish. Steadying my housing, I focused on 1-2 specs, no bigger than pinheads. Behold the results. Amazing? Truly.
These are a damsel fish, and as you can see, nearly clear-only their eyes and helmet are somewhat opaque and developed. The rest isn't finished!

THE LITTLE CREATURES

WORLD WITHIN A WORLD

Hermit crabs have eyes like a fly and some have very long eyelashes!

Even more fascinating is the clear covering over the eyes- almost like a built in Scuba mask found on all the eyes of underwater critters!

WORLD WITHIN A WORLD

Despicable Me

A close up of Sergeant Major eggs reveals two eyes, a dotted tail and a red tummy.

Dragonets are about as long as your pinky finger. With the 105mm they are adorable and often expressive subjects.

Notice the clear covering over the eyes (to the right). The built in scuba mask. But also revealed is the skin covering, stippled in millions of brownish color sensors. These may allow the animal to change it's coloring. Close ups with the 10x diopter reveal many fish have this stippling.

WORLD WITHIN A WORLD

Behold the details of the patterns and colors revealed with super macro close up. Here, we see a sample of mating or territorial color markings of a Lancer's Dragonet.

Close up of a Diamond Pipefish, *Syngnathidae*

Close up of a Banded Coral Shrimp -to the right is a close up of the face. Even they have a micro clear protection over their little eyes.

WORLD WITHIN A WORLD

The eyes of an Arrow crab show such unusual detail.

Baby Sharpnose Puffer, *Cathigaster rostrata Once again we can see the stipling effect that is most likely their color sensors*

WORLD WITHIN A WORLD

Leech aglaja, *Chelidonura hirundinina* Close up reveals a brushy face. A type of headshield slug, perhaps no bigger than an inch long.

Close up of Night Shrimps- check out the blade action front & center!

Blade Runners. Shrimp are definitely armed to the gills to do battle, here you can also see they have a forked tongue.

WORLD WITHIN A WORLD

Shrimp have the eyes to see from nearly all sides . . resembling a fly's eyes.

The Little People

SKELETON SHRIMP

Almost humanistic in appearance, except for the extraordinary long torso . . . okay and claws... and antennae. Often no bigger than an eyelash, these bizarre creatures live a social life much like people, in clans and can be found in the hydroids. The females carry babies in the belly, then once hatched, they carry them on their shoulders until mature enough to go out on their own. They seem to be quite acrobatic, throw wild dance parties, love to box and at times, the alpha males seem quite aggressive toward the females. ...If you look on the lower branch above, you can see a couple of the kids. Looks like Dad is giving them a lesson.

Caprella sp.

Females carry egg sacs on their belly and although these two gals are apparently from the same clan (notice the markings on the claws), they have different colored belly sacs.

PHOTO TIP:

The trick to photographing these, is to sit very still and observe and focus your own eyes on their movement or activity. Then gradually come in closer and closer until you can see their eyes. Without the eye contact, they just look like weeds.

The next thing that is important is to focus and determine which one is the alpha male. They are usually the largest one in the bunch, and the colony revolves around the big boss. The pregnant female is usually nearby (most likely for protection).

SKELETON SHRIMP

Skeleton Shrimp are actually amphipods, and not true shrimp. They strongly resemble grasshoppers from a scientific standpoint.

Each individual is as different as can be from one colony to another

PHOTO TIP:

Once you've found your subject, wait for them to move into an area with a plain background to set them apart, Then wait for your moment. If you are able to use a higher diopter or stack with a 1.4 teleconverter, you will be happier with the results.

A female with babies all over the place.

Dance Party

This looked like a party going on, or a family dance.

This skeleton shrimp has captured something with eyes, and is devouring it. Puts a whole new slant on the term "sucking face," doesn't it?

How many Skeleton shrimp can you find in the hydroids here to the left?

You might need a magnifying glass. But below you can see with the 10x subsee diopter there is an adult male, a juvenile below and from the looks of those antennae- probably an alpha male hiding behind stalk number 3... and woops, cut off the one on the upper left behind another polyp.

Are your eyes trained yet?

WORLD WITHIN A WORLD

OMG ! ! !   "Oh my goodness!"
One of the more incredible moments, is that moment of realization.... that is to say, when the animal the size of an eyelash realizes it is being watched and let's out that silent scream upon its discovery of the alien creature watching him (the photographer). And that an animal the size of an eyelash has feelings, emotions, a family, and throws really great parties has realized . . . it is not alone in this world.

So one has to ponder, would we make the same face? Most certainly.
Key to this image, if your eyes don't see it readily... look for the red eyes, the black mouth, nostrils, the clubbed mitts and antennae. Many international uw photographers are now stacking lenses in order to get those super close up shots.

The Bokeh (soft) background makes this Sea Star pastel shades of orange

The swirls and frills of a moon jelly mimic the delicate petals of an orchid

CAPTURING THE MOMENT

This chapter is dedicated to inspiration. Capturing a moment can be anything that incites an emotional feeling. Art is in the eye of the beholder. But what inspires this? It can be anything from dazzling beautiful colors and patterns to capturing a moment that we may only see once in a lifetime. While photographing, try to look beyond the obvious. Find the beauty in nature, whatever that may be to you, don't hold back. Evolve your abilities, your eye and your images.

The following images are a few idea shots and to reflect possibilities

CAPTURING THE MOMENT

While they Sleep

Fiiiiggaarrro !

CAPTURING THE MOMENT

Sincerity

The Dolphin Smile

CAPTURING THE MOMENT

"We are family . . . all my sisters and me"

The Horseman

Yes, fish have feelings

You Talkin to Me?

CAPTURING THE MOMENT

Muck Surfing

Fashionista

CAPTURING THE MOMENT

Mardi Gras

Sincerity
Juvenile Sea Robin

Forecast:
Grumpy with a dash of flowers.

CAPTURING THE MOMENT

Ooh Baby ooh.
Or in Flounder speak, ooh- you can't catch me if you try
.... notice the flounder in the background, also oooo-ing.

Another Oh My Goodness moment. Observe and wait for a moment to occur that strikes your inner heart. When I see a shrimp making a gesture similar to what we do as humans, I am riveted.

Capturing humanistic emotions can really boost an image's importance to the viewer.

Here the shrimp looks devastated at being seen by another worldly creature . . . me.

The Usual Subjects

Anemones

Angelfish

Gobies

CARDINALFISH

Filefish

Barbfish

Nudibranchs & Sea S

PARROTFISH

Bass & Groupers

Octopus

BLENNIES

BUTTERFLYFISH

Sea Robins

CRABS

COWFISH

Feather Dusters

Damselfish

LIVE SHELLS

Angelfish

Blue Angelfish, *Holacanthus bermudensis*

Queen Angelfish, *Holacanthus ciliaris*

Townsend Angelfish, Hybrid: *Holacanthus bermudensis x Holacanthus ciliaris*

Rock Beauty , Adult *Holocanthus tricolor*

French Angel, *hint yellow eye leather.*..French Angel, Adult *Pomacanthus paru*

Gray Angelfish, *Pomacanthus arcuatus*

Blue Angel juvenile..note tail is yellow &
2nd blue bar has a curve

Queen Angel, Juvenile
The Queen has the crown

Townsend Angel, juvenile

Rock Beauty , Juvenile

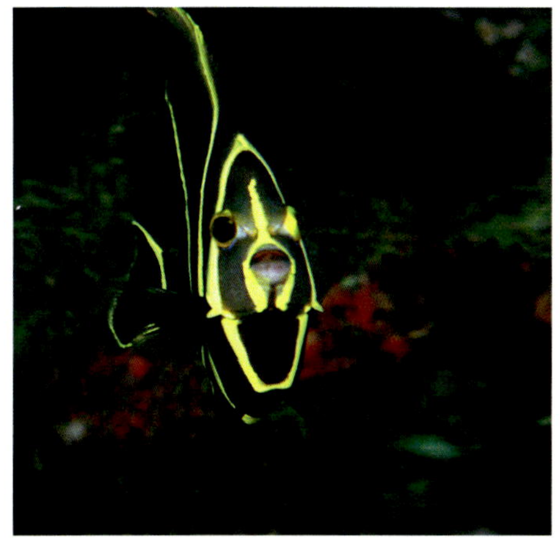

French Angel, juvenile

Gray Angel, Juvenile

Bass

Harlequin Bass, *Serranus tigrinus*

Dwarf Sand Perch, *Diplectrum bivvatum*

Lantern Sea Bass couple, *Serranus baldwini*

Bank Sea Bass, *Centropristis ocyurus*

Chalk Bass, *Serranus tortugarum*

Pygmy Sea Bass, *Serraniculus purnillo*

Bass / Grouper

Tiger Grouper, *Mycteroperca tigris* getting a teeth cleaning

Snowy Grouper juvenile, *Epinephelus niveatus*

Red Grouper juvenile, *Epinephelus morio*

Yellowmouth Grouper, *Mycteroperca interstitialis*

Graysby, *Epinephelus cruentatus*

Rock Hind, *Epinephelus adscensionis*

Black Sea Bass, *Centropristis striata*

Black Sea Bass standing his ground to the photographer.

Quite rarely seen... found on West side by the swim through and also on north side of east bridge

Fairy Basslet, *Gramma loreto*

Bass / Grouper/ Soapfish

Black Sea Bass, *Centropristis striata*

One of the most amazing realizations that can strike an underwater photographer is the often stupendous color variations that any sea creature may change to. Their personalities are equally fascinating as are their interactions to divers and underwater photographers.

Belted Sandfish, *Serranus subligarius*

Greater Soapfish, *Rypticus saponaceus*

Blackfin Blenny, *Paraclinus nigripinnis*

Banded Blenny, *Paraclinus fasciatus*

Rosy Blenny, *Malacoctenus macropus*

Rosy Blenny, *Malacoctenus macropus* Male variation

Downey Blenny, *Labrispmas kalisherae*

Rosy Blenny, *Malacoctenus macropus* Male variation

Blue Throat Pike Blenny, *Chaenopsis ocellata*

Yellowface Pike Plenny, *Chaenopsis limbaughi* (male)

Female Blue Throat Pike Blenny

Variations of the Hairy Blenny

Hairy Blenny, *Labrisoomus nuchipinnis*

Yes, all 4 animals here are the same . . a Hairy Blenny

The Male Hairy Blenny undergoes an amazing transformation during mating ritual. It changes from a mottled brownish coloration, to a rouge, then to this split orange with Black & White bodyfrom what you see on opposite page upper left to a tuxedo outfit bottom right.

Molly Miller; *Scarttella cristata*; combtooth blenny. Much like the Hairy blenny they are thicker and change colors to nearly black, to nearly light pink. If you are lucky you will get green & purple.

Roughhead Blenny, *Acanthemblemaria aspera*

Puff Cheek Blenny, *Labrisomus bucciferus*

Goldline Blenny, *Malococtenus aurolineatus* quite similar to a variation of the Saddled Blenny, but the dark bars meet between 2 & 3.

Saddled Blenny, *Malococtenus triangulatus*

Variations

Saddled Blenny, *Malococtenus triangulatus* Variation

Saddled Blenny, *Malococtenus triangulatus* Variation

Sailfin Blennies

Sailfin Blenny, *Emblemaria pandionis*, male

Sailfn blennies are very verbal, and while they are usually very small (about size of your pinky finger) if you just lie still and observe, you will witness a vast array of behaviors in a very short time. You just need to be patient. They will pop their sails in bursts of three. If you see this at a distance, stay absolutely still and ready your camera for the next outburst.

Sailfin Blenny, *Emblemaria pandionis*, female

They can change color at will, and do change from the normal navy blue/brownish color to green to a whitish color. These color variations occur when they are having a squirmish with one another. Could be territorial.

The standoff, or the battle for territorial rights... or a very strong argument

Seaweed Blennies

Seaweed blennies, *Parablennius marmoreus,* come in a variety of colors at the bridge. They are always good photo subjects with their expressive faces.

Try side lighting the gills to get that yellow inner glow.

Seaweed Blennies

BLENNY FACES

Tompot Blenny or Crested Blenny; *Hypleurochilus geminatus*

Butterflyfish

Spotfin
Butteflyfish, *Chaetodon ocellatus* juvenile. Last black mark will disappear to yellow in the adult.

Spotfin Butteflyfish, *Chaetodon ocellatus*

Banded Butterflyfish, *Chaetodon striatus*

Reef Butterflyfish, *Chaetodon sedentarius*

Foureye Butterflyfish, *Chaetodon capistratus*

CARDINAL FISH

Two Spot Cardinal fish, *Apogon pseudomaculatus*

Flamefish, *Apogon maculatus*, Adult above, juvenile below

Hermit Crabs

Red Striped Hermit Crab, *Phimochirus holthuisi*

Shortfinger Hermit, *Pagurus brevidactylus*

Tricolor Hermit, *Clibanarius tricolor*

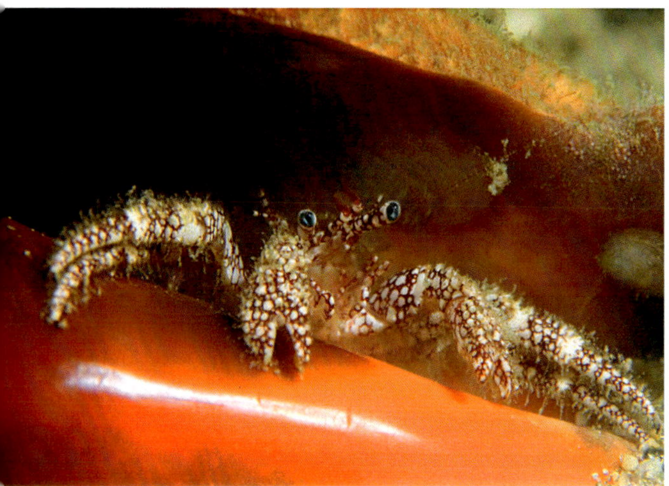

Whitespeckled Hermit, *Paguristes puncticeps*, exposed while seeking a larger shell for it's home.

Bareye Hermit, *Dardanus fucosus*

Polkadotted Hermit, *Phimochirus operculatus*

Hermit Crabs

Blue Eyed Hermit
Paguristes sericeus

Left handed, Blue eyed, golden-orange eye stalks

Hairy Hermit Crab,
Undetermined.
Rare

I love the red rhinestones coming down the arm

Giant Hermit
Petrochirus diogenes

CRABS

Sargassum Swimming Crab, *Portunis sayi*

Redhair Swimming Crab, *Achelous ordwayi*

Blackpoint Sculling Crab, *Cronius ruber*

Flatface Swimming Crab
Achelous depressifrons

Red Porcelain Crab
Petrolisthes marginatus

Yellow Box crab,
Calappa sulcataa

There are two embraced.

CRABS

Unknown Swimming Crab, *Portunus spinimanus sp*

Thinarm Clutch Crab, *Ebalia stimpsonii*

Shameface Heart Crab *Cryptosoma bairdi*

Decorator Crabs

Decorator Crabs are truly the punk rockers of the BHB. They take pride in their fashion statements! They show off their ability to co-habitate with living animals as a means of camouflage. To observe them is spectacular, especially at night when they come out in parade. To photograph them is quite another story. Best words of wisdom are to isolate the animal, make sure you get the eyes, and can see the claws.

Spongy Decorator Crabs
Macrocoeloma trispinosum

Roughnose Decorator Crab, *Leptopsia setirostris*

CRABS

Consider how amazing it is, that animals co-exist in this manner. They begin small and start adding pieces of living other animals to their body, as clothing, protection, color and spice. Its truly fascinating.

Shortfinger Neck Crab, *Podochela sidneyi*

Green Algae Crab, *Thersandrus compressus*

If you simply lie still on the sandy bottom, suddenly everything comes to life. Your job . . . capture the image.

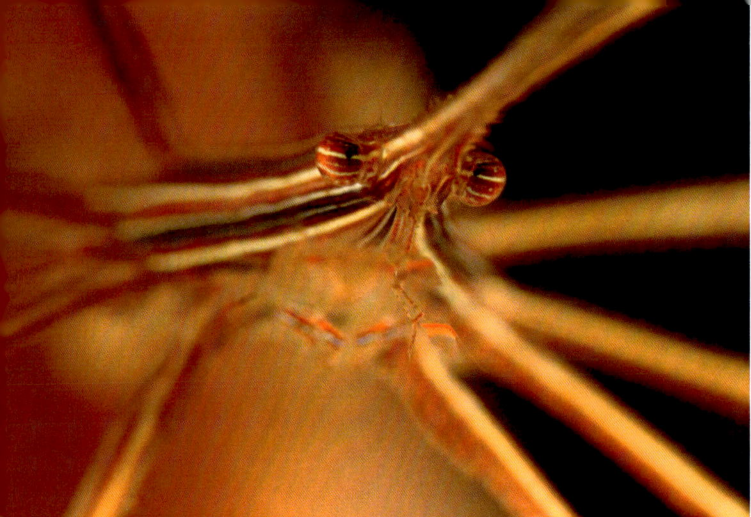

Yellowline Arrow Crab, *Stenorhynchus seticornis*
Also known as neck Crabs . . .close up taken with the 10x subsee to detail the eyes

Detail of the Eye of the Horseshoe Crab

Arrow crab eating something

Horseshoe Crab, *Limulus polyphemus*

Urchin Crabette -about size of a Bumblebee shrimp

Heart Urchin Pea Crab, *Dissodactylus primitivus*... notice this crab has incorporated a Pencil urchin quill into its body covering- and uses it as an extra leg.

In between a crab and a shrimp are these cute little rascals called Squat lobsters.

Bicolor Damselfish,
Stegastes partitus

Beaugregory,
Stegastes leucostictus
Juvenile

Cocoa Damselfish,
Stegastes variabilis
Juvenile
The notch at the base of the tail is the giveaway

These fish are so close its very difficult to tell them apart until you start counting notches and fins.

Beaugregory,
Stegastes leucostictus

Beaugregory,
Stegastes leucostictus

Cocoa Damselfish,
Stegastes variabilis

Yellowfin Chromis, *Chromis flavicauda*

Dusky Damselfish Juvenile, *Stegastes adustus* Juvenile

Blue Chromis, *Chromis cyanea*

DAMSELS

Sunshinefish Juvenile, *Chromis insolata*

Purple Reeffish, *Chromis scotti*

Sergeant Major, *Abudefduf saxatilis*

All Damsels are very territorial and quick to nip divers getting too close to their eggs, which they lay on flat open rocks. The Sgt. Majors turn a midnight blue color when defending a nest.

Dragonets

Lancer's Dragonet Male in full display
Paradiplogrammus bairdi

Lancer's Dragonet female in full display
Paradiplogrammus bairdi
Note shorter sailfin, lighter in color. Sometimes sailfin is black

Mating pair side by side. Blend into the sandy bottom very well. Tend to find in areas where there is a bit of an arena.

Fanworms & Feathers

Feather Dusters and Fan worms are everywhere, some are very small, but all are quite beautiful. Worth taking a close up to see what colorations it has. Avoid contact, many live in proximity to stinging hydroids.

Below, Star Horseshoe Worm, *Pomatostegus stellatus*

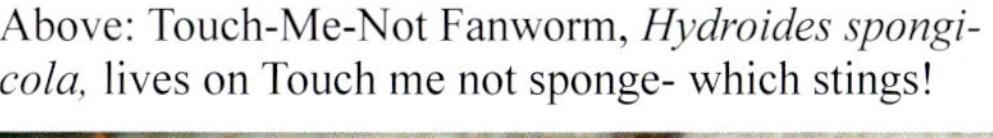

Above: Touch-Me-Not Fanworm, *Hydroides spongicola,* lives on Touch me not sponge- which stings!

Shy Featherduster, *Megalomma sp*

Red Spotted Horseshoe Worm, *Protula sp.*

Fanworms & Feathers

Fanworms have two eye stalks. If you nestle down and wait for one to open, you can observe them watching what goes by overhead. In order to observe you must not move a muscle.

California Horseshoe Worm, *Phoronopsis californica*

Brown Fanworm, *Notaulax nudicollis*

FILEFISH

Orange filefish,
Aluterus schoepfi

Rare sighting- passed through for a visit. Very inquisitive, and eager to bite off your nose. Very territorial, the school swam in defensive formation.

Unicorn filefish,
Aluterus monoceros

Found around the pilings

FILEFISH

Pygmy filefish, *Stephanolepsis setifer*

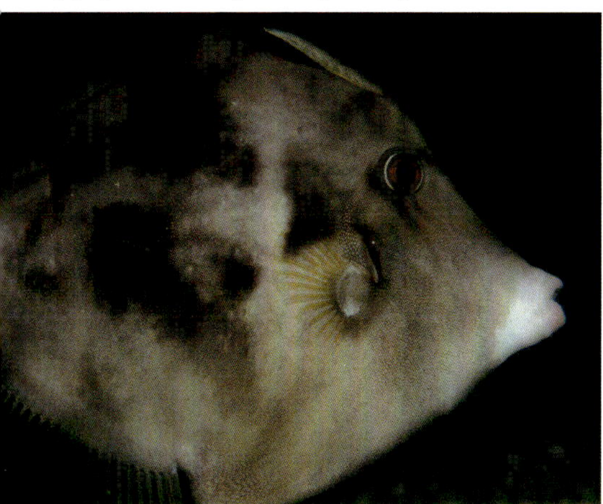

Planehead Filefish, *Stephanolepsis hsipidus* & juvenile to the right

Scrawled filefish, *Aluterus scriptus*

Eyed FLounder, *Bothus ocellatus* Close up of pattern

Eyed FLounder, *Bothus ocellatus*

FLOUNDER

Two Spot Flounder, *Bothus robinsiis*

Peacock Flounder, *Bothus lunatus*

Sargassumfish, *Histrio histrio*

Everyone wants a photo of them yawning! In actuality, I feel strongly that they do this as a warning guff- to let you know how big their mouth is, and is their way of asking you nicely to back off! You are too "in-their-space."

If you see one yawn or find one twirling it's lure - it will open its mouth, soon. So all you need to do is position yourself to be in the right place at the right time. That is of course without disturbing them from securing their morning breakfast.

Striated Frogfish, *Antennarius striatus*

The Dwarf Frogfish is ridiculously cute and adorable. Just a miniature version of the bigger Frogfish. Not juveniles.

All Frogfish are considered a prize shot. Take your time. Watch your lighting as those eyes can light up like a Christmas tree.

Dwarf Frogfish,
Antennarius pauciradiatus

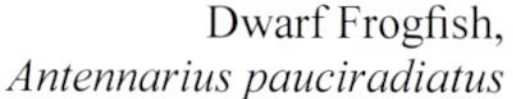

FROGFISH

Ocellated

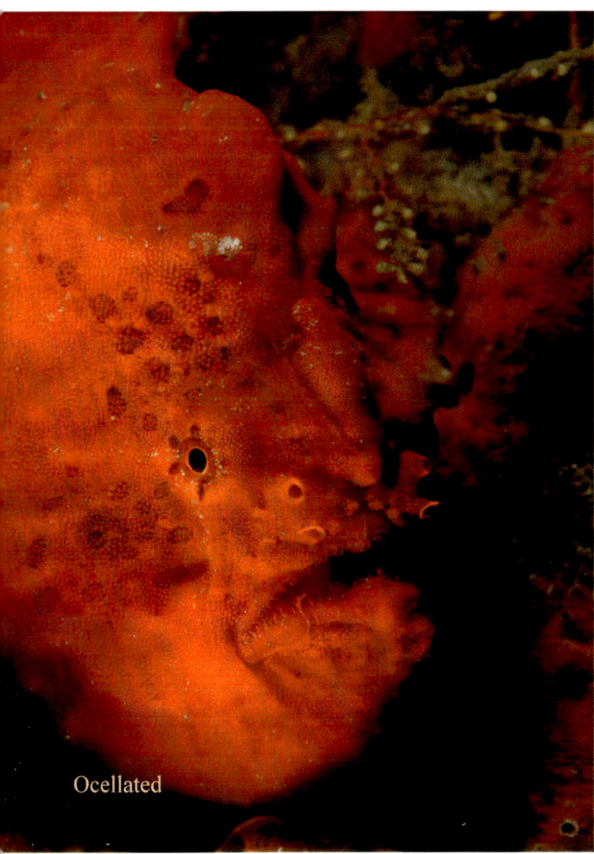

Ocellated

Frogfish at the BHB come in a variety of colors and types, and the color variances seem to change with each year that passes. For the longest time it seemed as though the main types we would see were the Striated, the black and the white one was a rare find. There has been rumor of a lavendar one, although I haven't seen that one yet... There are 4 types:
Striated
Ocellated
Dwarf
and the Sargassumfish.

The Striated aka Hairy Frogfish looks like it has army kackis on and is having a bad hair day!

The Dwarfs are very small found often in the calerpa sea grass beds.

The Sargassumfish has its own thing going on with really wild webbed feet with claws -and are normally found in the sargassum weed.

That means the rest are Ocellated.

Striated Frogfish - *Antennarius striatus*

Ocellated Frogfish - *Antennarius ocellatus*

Striated Frogfish - *Antennarius striatus*

FROGFISH

Ocellated Frogfish - *Antennarius ocellatus*

You may notice that they have an inordinate amount of sand on them. So . . . where do you think they hide?
Something to think about when pushing muck sticks into the sand, eh?

So... Fish with Feet? Hmmm, and yes they use them.

As our planet dips in and out of ice ages, the ocean levels rise and fall, and surviving species develop fins or legs, dependant on what is required for survival.

One has to ask, are they evolving back to land or back to water?

Striated Frogfish - *Antennarius striatus* juvenile

French Grunts are known for their red mouthed silent scream *Haemulon flavolineatum*

The prized shot is to get two in a face off.

French Grunt, juvenile, *Haemulon flavolineatum*

Cottonwick, Juvenile, *Haemulon melanurum*

Porkfish -juv, *Anisotremus virginicus*

Pluma, *Calamus pennatula*

Banner Goby Mating Pair; *Microgobius microlepsis*

Kuna Goby, *Coryphopterus kuna*

Seminole Goby, *Microgobius carri*

Dash Goby, *Ctenogobius saepepallens*

Banner Goby; M*icrogobius microlepis*

Tiger Goby, *Gobiosoma macrodon*

Blue Goby, *Ioglossus callirus*

Hovering Dartfish, *Ptereleotris helenae*

Colon Goby, *Coryphopterus dicrus*

Goldspot Goby, *Gnatholepsis thompsoni*

Bridled Goby, *Coryphopterus glaucofraenum*

Spotted Goby, *Coryphoterus punctipectophous*

Butter Hamlet, *Hypoplectrus unicolor*

Hamlet juvenile, *Hypoplectrus sp*

Barred Hamlet, *Hypoplectrus puella*

Hybrid Hamlet, perhaps part Tan Hamlet and Barred Hamlet

Yellowbelly Hamlet, *Hypoplectrus aberrans*

Blue Hamlet, *Hypoplectrus gemma*

MANATEES

Florida Manatees (*Trichechus manatus latirostrus*) are protected animals. They are on the Critically endangered species list by the IUCN. It is illegal to harass them. They do not normally seek human interaction at Blue Heron Bridge. On a lighter note, it is amazing to just observe them side by side, should you find one by chance. To be in the presence of a 600 lb mammal commands our intelligence and respect. Sadly, their encroaching extinction is as a direct result of mankind's impact on their domain. Boat strikes are the number one cause of death. However, they also cannot tolerate water temperatures below 68 ° f. In 2010 over 200 manatees perished due to colder waters. There are only around 3,000 left in Florida.

LIVE SHELLS - MOLLUSKS

Atlantic Sundial, *Architectonica perspectiva*

Colorful Moon Snail, *Naticarius canrena*

Atlantic Partridge Tun Shell, *Tonna Pennata*

Razor Clam, *Stubby solecurtus*, -open and airing out the bi-valves or feeding.

Asian Green Mussel, (Invasive species)

White Nassa, *Nassarius albus*

Scallop hunting at night

Thistle Scallop, *Lindapecten exasperatus*

West Indian Fighting Conch. *Strombus pugilis*

Florida Rock snail,
Stramonita haemastoma floridana

Milk Conch, *Strombus costatus*

Florida Horse Conch, *Pleuroploca gigantea*

Atlantic Thorny Oyster, *Spondylus americanus*

A great website for Shells is the Jaxshells.org
This is just a small sampling.

Rough Fileclam, *Ctenoides scabra*

Leech aglaja, *Chelidonura hirundinina* a headshield slug.

Pleurobranchus crossei, Sidegill slug found on a bottle

Pleurobranchus crossei, Sidegill slug

Lined Flatworm, *Maritigrella crozieri*

Pseudobiceros caribbensis

Inconspicuous pleurobranch, *Pleurobranchaea inconspicua*

Phidiana lynceus

Cratena perigrina cf. eating its favorite hydroid... note the orange cheek marks.

Felimida clenchi aka Harlequin Sea Goddess

Felimida binza laying eggs, does not have the pointed crowning design like the Clenchi to the left.

While these two are very similar in color, their patterns are quite different.

NUDIBRANCHS & SEA SLUGS

Flabellina marcusorum

Flabellina non specific

Flabellina verta - note the white marking

Flabellina Dushia, Common at BHB

There have been over 100 species of nudibranchs, sea slugs, and sea hares found at the Blue Heron Bridge. A great source of information can be found in the "Caribbean Sea Slugs" field guide by Valdés, Hamann, Behrens, DuPont.

Felimare ruthae, Gold lined Sea Goddess

Hypselodoris fregona possible sp 3

Learchis evelinae

(Above) I.D. uncertain, possibly a *Learchis evelinae* or a type of Cuthona. Very small -tip of your fingernail.

Miniature melo, *Micromelo undatus*

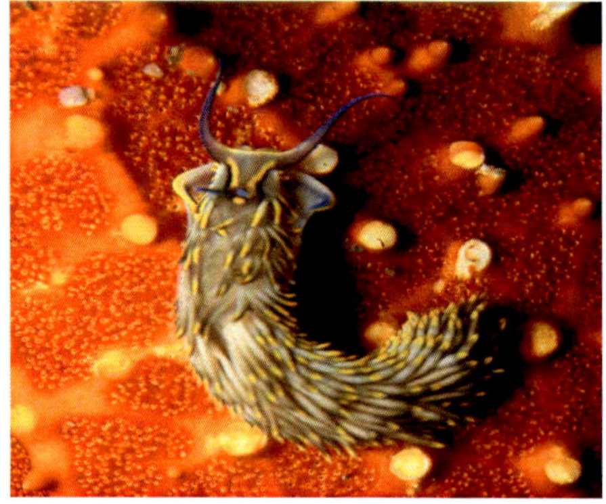

Cerberilla potiguara

Spurilla creutzberg

Favorinus auritulus, Long Eared Favorinus

Dondice occidentalis, Fringeback Dondice

Dondice occidentalis, Fringeback Dondice

Elysia ornata

Oxynoe antillarum

Ragged Sea Hare, about the size of a bunny, *Bursatella leachii.* You will often see two trailing one another

Mottled Seahare, *Aplysia brasiliana*

Striated Seahare, *Stylocheilus striatus*

Cuthona caerulea

Doto varaderoensis

Plocamopherus lucayansis-side view

P*locamopherus lucayansis* - head detailing the "face" & rhinophores

Lobiger souverbii

Frosty Mordilla, *Noumeaella kristenseni*

Lomanotus vermiformis

Rostanga byga

OCTOPUS & SQUID

Caribbean Reef Squid, *Sepioteuthis sepioidea*

Inverted squid displaying syphon with electric pulsation

Common Octopus, *Octopus vulgaris*

Juvenile Caribbean Reef, *Octopus briareus*

Reef octopus, "tenting" -night feeding, notice they change colors drastically when feed, in defense mode or mating

Brownstripe octopus, *Octopus burryi*

Rainbow Parrotfish, *Scarus guacamaia*

Queen Parrotfish, *Scarus vetula*

Stoplight Parrotfish, *Sparisoma viride*

Stoplight Parrotfish, *Sparisoma viride*, Supermale

Bucktooth Parrotfish, *Sparisoma radians*

Redband Parrotfish, *Sparisoma aurofrenatum*

PIPEFISH

Chain Pipefish, *Sygnathus louisianae*

Whitenose pipefish, *Cosmocampus albirostris*

Sargassum pipefish, *Syngnathus pelagicus*

Shortfin Pipefish, *Cosmocampus elucens*

American crested pipefish,

Diamond Pipefish, unidentified

PUFFERFISH

Balloonfish, *Diodon holocanthus*

Bandtail Pufferfish, *Sphoeroides spengleri*

Sharpnose Puffer, *Canthigaster rostrata*

Checkered Puffer, *Sphoeroides testudineus*

Above,:Webb Burrfish, *Chilomycterus antillarum*

Right: Striped Burrfish, *Chilomycterus schoepfi*

Bottom Right: Spotted Burrfish, *Chilomycterus atringa*

PERCH - RAZORFISH

Sand Perch, *Diplectrum formosum*

Sand Perch, *Diplectrum formosum*

Dwarf Sand Perch *Diplectrum bivittatum*

Green Razorfish, *Xyrichthys splendens*

Green Razorfish, *Xyrichthys splendens*

Slippery Dick, *Halichoeres bivittatus* eating a crab on the go...

Red Orange Ghost Shrimp, *Corallianassa longiventris.*. Rare and considered a great find!

Dark Mantis, *Neogonodactylus curacaoensis*

Ciliated False Squilla, *Pseudosquilla ciliata*

False squilla; *Pseudosquilla ciliata*

Golden Mantis, *Lysiosquilloides mapia.* A Rare find

Tiger Mantis, *Lysiosquilla maculata*

SHRIMP

Arrow Shrimp, *Tozeuma carolinense,* Broken Back Shrimp

Phyllognathia simplex, no bigger than a sliver of a finger nail. A rare rare find.

Unknown Broken-back shrimp, perhaps *Latreutes*

Slender Sargassum Shrimp, *Latreutes fucorum*

Shrimp are amazing. They come in all shapes, sizes, colors. . . you name it. Best time to see them in action is on a night dive, and the darker the better. They breakdown into about 6 -7 categories:
Boxer Shrimp
Broken Back Shrimp (Arrow, Sargassum)
Commensal Shrimp (clear shrimp, also may have 1 enlarged claw)
Gnathophyllidae (Bumblebee shrimp)
Hinge Beak Shrimp
Roughback Shrimp (fuzzy wuzzy's)
Snapping Shrimp (giant left claw)

Brown Grass Shrimp (Commensal Shrimp) Golden variation, *Leander tenuicournis*

Brown Grass Shrimp (Commensal Shrimp) Blue variation, *Leander tenuicournis*

Brown Grass Shrimp (Commensal Shrimp) Blue variation, *Leander tenuicournis*

Brown Grass Shrimp (Commensal Shrimp) orange variation, *Leander tenuicournis*

Banded Coral Shrimp, *Stenopus hispidus* (Boxer Shrimp)

Golden Coral Shrimp, *Stenopus scutellatus*

SHRIMP

These clear shrimp are found in the white hydroids and are practically invisible to the naked eye

Iridescent Shrimp Complex, *Periclimenes spp,* Commensal Shrimp

Red Snapping Shrimp, *Alphaeus armatus*

Unknown night shrimp

Below:
A closer view of a prawn shows us intense weaponry and a forked tongue! Many shrimp have blades such as these below.

Pink Spotted Shrimp, (Prawn) *Farfantepenaeus brasiliensis*

Close up of Night Shrimp

Roughback Shrimp, *Trachycaris rugosa*

Roughback Shrimp, *Trachycaris rugosa*

Pederson's Cleaner Shrimp, *Ancylomenes pedersoni,* Commensal Shrimp

Spotted Cleaner Shrimp, *Periclemenes yucatanicus*

Striped Bumblebee Shrimp, *Gnathophyllum americanum*

Striped Bumblebee Shrimp, *Gnathophyllum americanum*

WORMS

Bobbitt Worm, *Eunice aphrodite sp*

Fringed Worm, *Cirratulus grandis*

Ornate Scale Worm, polychaete worm undetermined

Peanut Worm, *Phylum Sipuncula*

Star Horseshoe Worm, *Pomatostegus stellatus*

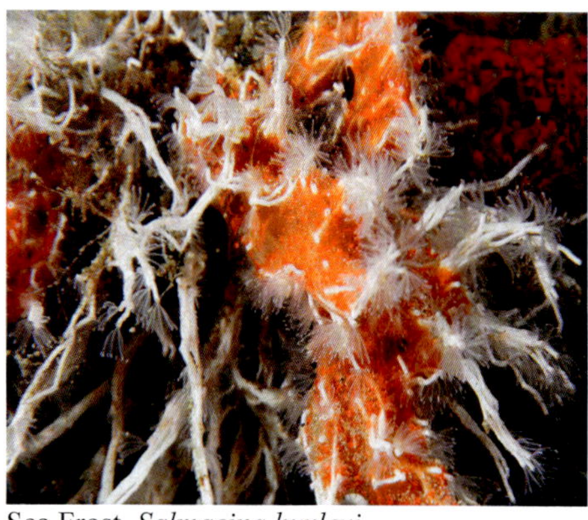

Sea Frost, *Salmacina huxleyi*

Yellowhead Wrasse juvenile, *Halichoeres garnoti*

Puddingwife newborn (less than 1")

Puddingwife juvenile (approx 2") *Halichoeres radiatus*

Black Ear Wrasse, *Halichoeres poeyi*

Clown Wrasse juv, *Halichoeres maculipinna*

Bluehead Wrasse Thalassoma bifasciatum

Hogfish, *Lachnolaimus maximus* They can change color to a deep hot pink < ---------------->

INDEX